Brian W. Aldiss

Twayne's English Authors Series

Kinley Roby, Editor

Northeastern University

TEAS 555

BRIAN ALDISS
Jerry Bauer

Brian W. Aldiss

Tom Henighan

Carleton University

Twayne Publishers
New York

Twayne's English Authors Series No. 555

Brian W. Aldiss
Tom Henighan

Twayne Publishers
1633 Broadway
New York, NY 10019

Library of Congress Cataloging-in-Publication Data

Henighan, Tom.
    Brian W. Aldiss / Tom Henighan.
        p.   cm. — (Twayne's English authors series ; no. 555)
    Includes bibliographical references and index.
    ISBN 0-8057-1601-7 (alk. paper)
    1. Aldiss, Brian Wilson, 1925 –   —Criticism and interpretation.
2. Science fiction, English—History and criticism.   I. Title.
II. Series: Twayne's English authors series ; TEAS 555.
PR6051.L3Z69   1999
823'.914—dc21   99-12255
                                                            CIP

This paper meets the requirements of ANSI/NISO Z3948-1992 (Permanence of Paper).

10 9 8 7 6 5 4 3 2 1

Printed in the United States of America

To Judith Merril (1923–1997),
distinguished anthologist and indefatigable enthusiast of SF

Contents

Preface

When I undertook this study of the work of Brian Aldiss, other subjects laid claim to a considerable part of my research time. Nonetheless, it was a pleasure to revisit the many Brian Aldiss books I knew and to be given the opportunity to consider other works by this prolific writer, titles familiar to me only by name that in the end proved to be very well worth exploring.

Although Brian Aldiss's work has been the subject of some intelligent critical attention, most of it is outdated—he has gone on publishing important works into the 1990s—and is in any case marked by too much special pleading. Just because his work has been unfairly neglected, it has attracted strong advocacy, yet perhaps it can be better served at this point by a steadier overview. Previous books on Aldiss, for example, praise his experimental works at the expense of his more conventional fiction and celebrate *Frankenstein Unbound* for its intellectual content without taking into account its deficiencies as a novel. My evaluation is different, although I consider some of Aldiss's intertextual fiction to be among his best. We have come a long way since the new wave and the *nouveau roman,* and it is possible to see those phenomena in perspective, without inflating their importance in either the history of science fiction or in the story of twentieth-century literature in general. Aldiss's best works, I believe, are original in ways that are subtle and quietly effective. The experimental works, however interesting, seem to have dated. To me, Aldiss's career offers yet another confirmation that—as an American music critic once neatly put it—what is merely *à la mode* tends to become quickly outmoded.

Aldiss has many literary achievements to his credit, but one of the most interesting aspects of his work has been his ability to move back and forth between speculative fiction and the so-called mainstream. Very few science fiction writers could aspire to be serious candidates for the Booker Prize, for example, yet Aldiss was at least once strongly touted for that distinction, although he was not actually nominated. (He did function as a Booker Prize judge, however.) Aldiss also happens to be the author of some remarkable short stories and of a history of science fiction that at one stroke demolished nearly half a century's parochial readings of the genre. Thanks to *Billion Year Spree,* a reluctant fandom was compelled to see science fiction from a sharper perspective, while outside critics were encouraged to rethink the place of science fiction within the wider traditions of western literature.

Beginning in the mid-1970s and continuing for several years thereafter, I taught a course in science fiction at Carleton University in Ottawa, which, as the critic Judith Merril noted, was one of the first courses of its kind in Canada. This course culminated in a memorable 1978 conference that brought together scientists and science fiction writers, academics and the public for several days of speculation and exchange on important issues. Frank Herbert, John Brunner, Edgar Mitchell (the sixth man to walk on the moon), Judith Merril, John Chapman (the founding father of the Canadian space program), Gerhard Herzberg (a Nobel prizewinning chemist), and Darko Suvin, critic and theorist, were among the notables who participated. In those days, although my thoughts were much taken up with speculation about science and society, I had small acquaintance with the work of Brian Aldiss, one of the real masters of this particular form of the science fiction genre. One of the reasons was the unavailability of Aldiss's works, a situation that still applies to many of the most important science fiction writers, who must wince as they witness the occlusion of science fiction by the seemingly endless proliferation of heroic fantasy on bookstore shelves.

It is time that some enterprising publisher took up the implicit challenge to issue (and keep in print!) a series of the key science fiction works of the century in uniform format, so that a new reading public can get a sense of the brilliant work done in this genre, much of it unavailable even in public libraries. I'm convinced that if such a series were launched, several of Brian Aldiss's novels would be immediate candidates for inclusion.

Acknowledgments

This book would have been impossible without the assistance of others. I have to thank Carleton University for a small grant that helped fund some of the basic research. Brian McLeod, one of my graduate students, dug deeply into Aldiss—especially the *Helliconia* books—and many of his insights contributed to this study. Erin Robinson, who has worked with me on other projects, proved again to be a wonderful research assistant. Graduate students Jason Mattless and Sue Globensky did some valuable eleventh-hour searching. I want to thank also the Carleton University Interlibrary Loans Department for obtaining some hard-to-get Aldiss material. The Merril Library in Toronto was also very helpful, and I want to mention especially Mary Cannings for some timely phone advice. Thanks go also to John Park, a science fiction writer himself, for offering to lend me Aldiss books and to the Science Fiction Society of Ottawa for inviting me more than once to talk about Aldiss. I would like to thank my wife, Marilyn, for her patience during busy times and my son, Michael, for sharing some of his Aldiss readings with me.

This study would have been almost impossible, however, without the work of the late Margaret Aldiss, whose *The Work of Brian W. Aldiss: An Annotated Bibliography and Guide* (1992; still available from the Borgo Press in San Bernardino, California) is a foundation for all present and future Aldiss study. Finally, I want to thank all the students of my old English 207 course for helping me get a deeper grounding in the science fiction I had first discovered as a child and for a long time neglected and also Professor Douglas Barbour of the University of Alberta for showing the way to writers and teachers of speculative fiction in Canada. My final debt, to Judith Merril, a great editor and an indefatigable promoter of science fiction, is expressed in the dedication.

Permission to quote from the following material has been granted by Robert Reginald and Borgo Press: Margaret Aldiss, *The Work of Brian W. Aldiss: An Annotated Bibliography and Guide,* ed. Boden Clarke (San Bernardino, Calif.: R. Reginald, Borgo Press, 1992); Michael R. Collings, *Brian W. Aldiss* (Mercer Island, Wash.: Starmont House, 1986); Richard Mathews, *Aldiss Unbound: The Science Fiction of Brian W. Aldiss* (San Bernardino, Calif.: Borgo Press, 1977).

Chronology

1957   Becomes literary editor for the *Oxford Mail* newspaper (through 1969). Publishes *Space, Time, and Nathaniel.*

1958   Named "Most Promising New Author of the Year" at sixteenth World Science Fiction Convention (Solacon). Publishes *Non-Stop.*

1959   Caroline Wendy Aldiss, second child, born 8 March. Publishes *Vanguard from Alpha* and *The Canopy of Time.* Receives "Most Promising New Author" award at World Science Fiction Convention.

1960   Cofounds Oxford University Speculative Fiction Group with C. S. Lewis. Publishes *Bow Down to Nul* and a collection of linked stories, *Galaxies Like Grains of Sand.*

1961   Appointed editor of the Penguin Science Fiction Series (through 1964). Publishes *The Male Response; Penguin Science Fiction;* and *The Primal Urge.*

1962   Wins Hugo Award for best short fiction of 1961 for the *Hothouse* series. Publishes *Hothouse* and *Best Fantasy Stories.*

1963   Publishes *The Airs of Earth* and *More Penguin Science Fiction.*

1964   Travels through Yugoslavia for six months with Margaret Manson to research his travel book *Cities and Stones.* Publishes *The Dark Light Years; Greybeard; Yet More Penguin Science Fiction; Introducing SF;* and *Starswarm.* Edits and publishes a critical magazine, *SF Horizons,* with Harry Harrison (through 1965).

1965   Divorced from Olive Fortescue. Marries Margaret Christie Manson on 11 December. The Aldisses move to Jasmine House, Wheatley. Guest of honor at twenty-third World Science Fiction Convention (Loncon II). Publishes *Best Science Fiction Stories of Brian W. Aldiss; Earthworks;* and *SF Horizons 2.*

1966   Wins Nebula Award for best novella of 1965, "The Saliva Tree." Publishes *The Saliva Tree and Other Strange Growths* and *Cities and Stones: A Traveller's Jugoslavia.*

1967   Timothy Nicholas Aldiss, third child, born 5 August. Publishes *An Age* and *Nebula Award Stories Two* (with

Harry Harrison). Helps obtain an Arts Council grant for the magazine *New Worlds*.

1968   The Aldisses move to Heath House, Southmoor. Publishes *Report on Probability A; Best SF: 1967* (with Harrison); and *Farewell, Fantastic Venus!* (with Harrison). Becomes art correspondent for *The Guardian*.

1969   Charlotte May Aldiss, fourth child, born 8 March. Guest at the Science Fiction Festival in Rio de Janeiro, Brazil. Publishes *Barefoot in the Head; Intangibles Inc. and Other Stories; Best SF: 1968* (with Harrison); and *A Brian Aldiss Omnibus.* Voted "Britain's most popular science fiction writer" by the British Science Fiction Association.

1970   The Tokyo International Science Fiction Symposium established at Aldiss' suggestion. Publishes *The Hand-Reared Boy; Neanderthal Planet; Best SF: 1969* (with Harrison); *The Shape of Further Things;* and *The Moment of Eclipse.* Received a Ditmar Award as the world's best contemporary science fiction author for the year.

1971   Publishes *A Soldier Erect;* the revised edition of *Best Science Fiction Stories of Brian Aldiss; Best SF: 1970* (with Harrison); and *A Brian Aldiss Omnibus,* vol. 2.

1972   Publishes *The Book of Brian Aldiss; Best SF: 1971* (with Harrison); and *The Astounding-Analog Reader,* vol. 1 (with Harrison). Wins the British Science Fiction Award for *The Moment of Eclipse.*

1973   Publishes *Frankenstein Unbound; Best SF: 1972* (with Harrison); *The Astounding-Analog Reader,* vol. 2 (with Harrison); *The Penguin Science Fiction Omnibus;* and *Billion Year Spree,* a history of the science fiction genre.

1974   Publishes *The Eighty-Minute Hour: A Space Opera; Best SF: 1973* (with Harrison); *Space Opera;* and *Space Odysseys.*

1975   Becomes involved with the Society of Authors and invited to join its Committee of Management. Publishes *Best SF: 1974; SF Horizons; Hell's Cartographers; Decade: The 1940s* (all with Harrison); *Science Fiction Art;* and *Evil Earths.*

1976   Publishes *The Malacia Tapestry; Decade: The 1950s* (with Harrison); and *Galactic Empires.*

1977   Moves with family to Oxford. Elected chairman of the Society of Author's Committee of Management (through 1978). One of five writers officially invited to the Soviet Union. Publishes *Last Orders and Other Stories; Decade: The 1960s* (with Harrison); and *Brothers of the Head.* Wins the first James Blish Award for excellence in science fiction criticism.

1978   Appointed to the Arts Council Literature Panel (through 1980). Visits Sumatra and Singapore. Goes to Australia for Unicon IV. Wins Pilgrim Award for lifetime contributions to the study of science fiction. Publishes *A Rude Awakening; Perilous Planets; Science Fiction as Science Fiction;* and *Enemies of the System: A Tale of Homo Uniformis.*

1979   Moves with family to Orchard House, Begbroke. Visits the People's Republic of China. Guest of honor at the World Science Fiction Convention in London. Publishes *New Arrivals, Old Encounters; Science Fiction Verhalen; This World and Nearer Ones;* and *Pile: Petals from St. Klaed's Computer.*

1980   Invited to Singapore as guest writer for its annual book fair. Publishes *Moreau's Other Island* and *Life in the West.* Serves a term as chairman of the Cultural Exchanges Committee for the Society of Authors.

1981   Returns with family to Oxford. Appointed a judge of the Booker Prize. Publishes *Foreign Bodies* (in Singapore). First visit to annual IAFA Conference of the Fantastic in Boca Raton, Florida.

1982   Publishes *Helliconia Spring; Brian W. Aldiss: Dunkler Bruder Zukunft: Der Brian W. Aldiss-Reader;* and *Farewell to a Child: 10 Poems.* Becomes a founding trustee of World Science Fiction. Institutes the annual World Science Fiction awards.

1983   Wins John W. Campbell Memorial Award for *Helliconia Spring.* Becomes president of World Science Fiction (through 1984). Anthony Burgess chooses *Life in the*

West as one of the best 99 novels published in the English language since 1939. Publishes *Helliconia Summer; Best of Aldiss;* and *Science Fiction Quiz.* Chairman of World Science Fiction annual meeting in Zagreb, Yugoslavia.

1984   The Aldisses move to large Edwardian house, Woodlands, on Boars Hills outside of Oxford. Publishes *Seasons in Flight.*

1985   Publishes *Helliconia Winter; The Book of Mini-Sagas I; The Pale Shadow of Science;* and an autobiographical essay in *Contemporary Authors Autobiography Series* (vol. 2). Chief guest at Centre d'Etude de la Metaphore Colloque, Nice, France. Guest at Toronto Harbourfront Literary Festival.

1986   Publishes . . . *And the Lurid Glare of the Comet; The Penguin World Omnibus of Science Fiction* (with Sam J. Lundwall); *Trillion Year Spree* (with David Wingrove). Guest of honor at Helsinki Science Fiction Convention.

1987   Publishes *Ruins; The Year Before Yesterday* (his hundredth monograph); and *The Magic of the Past.* First performance of *Science Fiction Blues.* Founds Avernus publishing house, with Frank Hatherley. Master of ceremonies at the forty-fifth World Science Fiction Convention at Brighton, England. Hugo Award for *Trillion Year Spree* (with David Wingrove).

1988   Publishes *Best Science Fiction Stories of Brian W. Aldiss* (revised collection; called *Man in His Time* in the United States); *Forgotten Life; The Book of Mini-Sagas II; Sex and the Black Machine;* and *Science Fiction Blues: The Show That Brian Aldiss Took on the Road,* performed throughout England and Germany.

1989   Publishes *A Romance of the Equator: Best Fantasy Stories.* Visits Egypt, San Marino for the World Science Fiction meeting, Bellagio, and Milano. Filming of Roger Corman's *Frankenstein Unbound.* Guest of honor at Moscon in Banff, Alberta, Canada. Also visits Toronto. His three-hundredth short story, "North of the Abyss," is published in *The Magazine of Fantasy & Science Fiction.*

1990   Edits *My Madness: The Selected Writings of Anna Kavan.*
       Publishes *Bury My Heart at W. H. Smith's: A Writing
       Life.* Attends IAFA Conference in March. Works with
       director Stanley Kubrick for six weeks on possible film
       script for "Super Toys." Visits Albania for *Marie Claire.*
       Attends NasCon in Stockholm, Sweden, and the 48th
       Worldcon in The Hague. Visits Singapore for *Daily
       Telegraph.* Release of Corman's *Frankenstein Unbound.*

1991   Publishes *Dracula Unbound.* Revisits China after 12
       years with a World Science Fiction group. Attends
       annual IAFA conference in Florida.

1992   Publishes *Remembrance Day.* Writes *Kindred Blood in
       Kensington Gore,* a short play. Attends annual IAFA con-
       ference in Florida.

1994   Publishes *Somewhere East of Life,* the final volume of the
       Squire Quartet (which includes *Life in the West, Forgotten
       Life,* and *Remembrance Day*).

1995   *The Secret of this Book* (published in the United States as
       Twenty Odd Stories); also published in United States *The
       Detached Retina: Aspects of Science Fiction and Fantasy.*

1998   Wife, Margaret Aldiss, dies. Publishes *The Twinkling of
       an Eye: My Life as an Englishman* and the first two vol-
       umes of a new edition of the Squire Quartet. An elabo-
       rate Brian Aldiss Web page is established, with sum-
       maries of nearly all of his books and full-color
       reproductions of the original jackets. A poll of readers
       establishes *The Moment of Eclipse* and *Barefoot in the Head*
       as favorite Aldiss texts.

1999   Completes *When the Feast is Finished,* an account of his
       wife's last illness and its effect on his family and him-
       self. Moves toward completion of a new major science
       fiction novel, tentatively titled *White Mars,* due for
       publication in 1999.

Chapter One
Brian Aldiss: A Writing Life

Early Life

Brian Wilson Aldiss was born 18 August 1925, in East Dereham, Norfolk, England. His mother was Elizabeth May Wilson, and his father was Stanley Aldiss, a tradesman with shops in East Dereham and Oxford and the son of a draper and the grandson of a blacksmith from Suffolk in East Anglia.[1] When Harry Hilyard Aldiss, Brian's grandfather, left his two sons the outfitting business he had started years before, Stanley decided to sell his share to his brother. As a result the family moved to Gorelston-on-Sea, where Brian attended St. Peter's Court Preparatory School, located in Bacton, some 20 miles away. Later, he moved on to Framlingham College, Suffolk, and finally, in 1939—when the family moved to the west country, to Devon—Aldiss was enrolled in West Buckland School, which he left in 1943 when he was drafted into the British army.

First memories of Brian Aldiss as a boy surface from his time at West Buckland School. One of the masters, Harold Boyer, recalls that Brian arrived "wearing short trousers and a benign smile," but adds that "the smile covered a load of mischief."[2] Aldiss began his literary career at West Buckland. Writing longhand with a flashlight under the bedclothes, he wrote poems, stories—mostly "pornographic crime" and science fiction—and satirical articles, some of which were in great demand among his classmates.[3] Aldiss's penchant for inventive wordplay surfaced early: in a debate on the motion "the English are a nation of hypocrites" young Brian argued that "England is a democracy, not a hypocracy!" And he described one of his salacious detective characters as going to New York "for a change of obscenery." Early influences on Brian Aldiss's imagination included the Disney-Stokowski *Fantasia*—primarily for its visual splendors—and J. W. Dunne's book, *An Experiment with Time,* which gave the young Aldiss a sense of the excitement of speculative thinking and stimulated his first grapplings with the time-problem that would become one of the main themes of his fiction.[4]

After only one year in the sixth form, Aldiss was drafted and sent off for several months of military training in England. At age 19, he was transferred overseas and served with the Royal Corps of Signals in India, Assam, Burma, Sumatra, Singapore, and Hong Kong. Photographs of the time show a tall, slender, dark-haired young man, with rather eager-looking but keenly humorous eyes peering out from behind thick spectacles. Aldiss kept in touch with his old schoolmates, writing detailed letters illustrated with pen and ink sketches. His military experience was to become the basis of several later novels and many stories, but his first professional writing was about the bookselling trade. After being decommissioned in 1947, Aldiss went to work for Sanders & Company Booksellers on High Street, Oxford—and later for Parker's—a time delightfully recalled in his first full-length work of fiction, *The Brightfount Diaries,* which appeared in 1955, under the prestigious imprint of Faber & Faber.

In 1948 Aldiss married Olive Fortescue, with whom he had two children. They were divorced in 1965, amid some contention and bitterness. Aldiss had fallen in love with Margaret Manson—she worked at the Royal Opera House, Covent Garden, and was no fan of science fiction—and he married her the year his divorce came through.[5] Margaret Aldiss soon became one of the authorities on Brian's published work and the author of several comprehensive bibliographies, as well as the mother of two subsequent Aldiss children. She died in 1998.

A Prolific Writer

Brian Aldiss became a full-time writer in 1956 and a veritable avalanche of creative writing ensued, nearly 100 published works in the first 15 years, with many more to follow. Aldiss was eventually to establish himself as one of the most energetic and versatile British writers of the century, inside science fiction or out, although his reputation did not always seem to reflect the high quality of his best work. But his career has been rich and various in many ways. For 12 years (from 1957 to 1969) he was literary editor of the *Oxford Mail;* from 1961 to 1964 he was editor of the Penguin Science Fiction Series. Later he was art correspondent for *The Guardian* (1968). Aldiss served on the Committee of Management of the Society of Authors (1975; chair in 1977); was appointed to the Arts Council Literature Panel from 1978 to 1980; and to the Booker Prize Committee (1981). From 1982 to 1984 he was president of World Science Fiction and instituted their annual awards. In 1987, with Frank

Hatherley, he founded the publishing house Avernus, and he remains an editorial adviser to the noted American critical journal *Extrapolation*.

An inescapable part of being a contemporary science fiction writer is the duty to take part in one or more aspects of the lively subculture associated with the genre.[6] To attend conventions, to serve on panels, to join debates, to correspond with fans and fanzines, to run workshops, even to give what amounts to vaudeville performances—such activities are almost obligatory, and the science fiction writer who tries to avoid them does so at the risk of being marginalized or forgotten. There was never any danger, it seems, of Brian Aldiss balking at this plunge into the world of science fiction conventions and fandom. From the beginning he has taken to it with zest, showing a flair for performance exceptional even among the most extroverted and voluble of British writers. His solid record as a prizewinning science fiction writer guaranteed him the opportunity to shine in this subculture; he has seized upon it with a relish and performed with a skill that relegates even his American counterpart Harlan Ellison to second place as "stage author." Aldiss's achievements in this theatrical vein range from brilliant improvisatory public conversation and monologues to an actual performance vehicle, *Science Fiction Blues: The Show That Brian Aldiss Took on the Road* (1988), performed with the actors Ken Campbell and Petronilla Whitfield.

The reality that anchors the showman, however, is Aldiss the much-honored convention guest, and especially Aldiss the editor and writer. His lifetime of prizes and honors include Most Promising New Author of the Year at the sixteenth World Science Fiction Convention (1958); a Hugo Award for stories from the *Hothouse* series (1962); guest of honor at the twenty-third World Science Fiction Convention (1965); a Nebula Award for his novella "The Saliva Tree" (1965); a Pilgrim Award for lifetime contribution to science fiction (1978); guest of honor at the World Science Fiction Convention (1979); the John W. Campbell Memorial Award for *Helliconia Spring* (1983); a Hugo award (shared with David Wingrove) for *Trillion Year Spree,* a revised and expanded edition of *Billion Year Spree,* Aldiss's extraordinary critical and historical study of 1973; guest of honor at the Helsinki Science Fiction Convention (1986); master of ceremonies at the forty-fifth World Science Fiction Convention (1987); and guest of honor at Moscon in Banff, Alberta, Canada (1989).

These awards and honors demonstrate Brian Aldiss's claim to a significant place in the development of British and world science fiction after 1945, but they only hint at his important connection with the changing role of science fiction in the postmodern era. Before we deal with this issue, however, it is necessary to track the trajectory of Aldiss's career a little more closely.

Aldiss's first full-length science fiction novel was *Non-Stop*, published in Britain in 1958 (and in the United States under the title *Starship* in 1959). This novel, a "generation starship" story that depicts life on a spaceship destined to travel to the stars, creates resonances with the traditional mythology of the eternal traveler and connects with postmodern starship stories emphasizing the theme of existential woe in space, such as the Nobel Prize winner Harry Martinson's narrative poem *Aniara*.[7] *Starship* set the tone for Aldiss's productions of the first half of the sixties, when he wrote novels of sensitivity and intelligence in the "social science fiction" vein.[8] In *Hothouse* (1962) and *Greybeard* (1964), in particular, Aldiss created exceptional stories about whole societies forced to deal with extraordinary changes in the physical world. The emphasis in these novels was not on the power of science itself to alter perspectives—nor did Aldiss waste much effort in buttressing his extrapolated stories with scientific theory; instead he focused on the unique and challenging qualities of the social order resulting from extraordinary change. This focus was criticized by some (James Blish, for example, in the case of *Hothouse*), and indeed it seemed to challenge the ground rules of "modern" science fiction laid down by the influential editor, John W. Campbell. In fact, these stories represented Aldiss's attempt to respond creatively to the "classic" science fiction of Wells and Stapledon, a not surprising choice for a British writer with an excellent knowledge of his own country's literary traditions.[9]

The New Wave

By the mid-sixties Aldiss seemed to have shifted gears. The new wave had burst upon the scene and some of his work was enlisted as part of the movement. In Judith Merril's *England Swings SF* (1968), the anthology that introduced new wave to American readers, she records a conversation with Aldiss in which he declares the movement to be "a publicity stunt," and in general disclaims its revolutionary status.[10] His retrospective view, however, as expressed in the essay "A Robot Tended Your Remains," frames the historical changes better: "Disenchantment or curiosity made many writers look away from space and the future to the world about them. . . . The sixties was the decade in which SF discovered the Present. It is no coincidence that it was also the decade in which the general reading public discovered SF."[11]

As for the literary experiments of the sixties, the truth is that Aldiss, from the beginning, was an experimenter, a writer eager to try new styles and forms, a man fascinated by language and word play. (Even *The Brightfount Diaries,* closer to *All Things Great and Small* than to Kafka, demonstrates a compulsive love of wordplay). It was natural for Aldiss to try his wings with the new movement, just as it was part of his nature to become associated with Michael Moorcock's forward-looking magazine *New Worlds,* for which he helped obtain an Arts Council grant in 1967. The same openness that made it possible for Aldiss to accept C. S. Lewis and his contributions to science fiction (despite the old-guard Oxfordian style of Lewis) allowed him to take part in, without being absorbed by, the experiments of the new wave.[12] Aldiss saw the sixties as a time of liberation. He was then in his forties, embarking on a second marriage, and just at the stage where many long for a new start in life and feel confident they can enrich themselves by making changes. As a science fiction writer, Aldiss (in common with many of his contemporaries) saw the drug culture and the new sexual freedom—not yet turned ambiguous or sinister—as part of the challenge to extend the boundaries of the genre. They saw the necessity—if their writing was to reflect contemporary reality—of taking science fiction inward.[13] They wanted to get away from technology and even from social extrapolation, to explore areas that were previously considered taboo areas. To take this step, however, they would need to extend their stylistics, they believed, in a way that would owe more to Joyce, Virginia Woolf, and William Burroughs than to H. G. Wells, Heinlein, or Asimov.

To understand this movement, some background is necessary.

As is well-known, the origins of science fiction are both complex and curious. While it is possible to trace the genre back to sources in the classical world, science fiction is inextricably connected with the rise of science in western society. A milestone—pointed to by Aldiss himself— is Mary Shelley's *Frankenstein* (1818), in which the protagonist renounces occult study for modern science at the instigation of one of his professors, M. Waldman. Waldman's paean to the powers of science sounds a prophetic note for the whole nineteenth century.[14] Thereafter, certain ingenious minds (Poe, Jules Verne, H. G. Wells, Olaf Stapledon) created a body of work in which the fantastic, or "romance," element of traditional fiction was reshaped in relation to scientific invention and theory, technology, and social transformation. Some of the old mythological themes of western literature were then reborn in a framework in which the principle of "alienation" controls the narrative.[15] Stories are created that transform reality in a way which reveals an estrangement from the present but which at the same time forms a link to it through the extrapolation of a scientific episteme (fact or known invention).[16] Whereas fantasy constructs its consistent imaginary worlds independent of any grounding in the reality of science and technology, the new literature of science fiction formed an uneasy but enduring relationship with that aspect of human psycho-social development and would be unthinkable without it.

In the nineties of the last century, when H. G. Wells was just beginning his long career, an ingenious American entrepreneur named Frank Munsey took American publishing in a new direction with the creation of the "pulps," cheap story magazines designed to tap into the market created by a vastly expanded reading public in the United States.[17] The diversification and specialization of the pulps resulted in the creation of "genre magazines" devoted to detective fiction, horror stories, westerns, and so on. One of the last genres to appear in this form was science fiction, which made its bow in the magazines published in New York in the twenties by Hugo Gernsback, an enterprising Belgian immigrant, a man with a keen appreciation of mechanical invention but little sense of the art of fiction.[18]

Gernsback's initial gesture was developed with far more consistency and business aplomb, and with superior literary and scientific awareness, by John W. Campbell, the longtime editor of Astounding Science Fiction, the magazine that set the tone for American science fiction of the thirties, forties, and fifties.[19] Campbell's editorship moved science fiction away from the improbable intellectual mixtures and crude narratives of the thirties magazines. He created an efficient if limited literature and nourished a very specific kind of science fiction subculture, one that valued honest writing but that remained indifferent to literary fiction. The typical Campbell story showed a self-confident relationship with the technology and science of the time (space travel, nuclear power), focusing on the human figure while at the same time dabbling in such outré matters as psi power and Dianetics. That an Astounding story by Heinlein, van Vogt, Asimov, or Poul Anderson, for example, had little of the symbolic power, little of the literary depth and originality of the stories of the nineteenth-century American practitioners of science fiction, was a matter of indifference to most fans, who in growing numbers both guyed and affirmed (but mostly affirmed) the values of the scientific miracles recounted in the magazine. In no sense, however, did the American science fiction written between 1930 and 1950 justify the hyperbole implicit in the term "golden age" that has often been applied to it.[20]

However important Campbell was as a transition figure, the revolution of the 1960s known as "new wave," which affected both British and American science fiction, can be understood as an effort to transcend Campbell's ideals and to realign the genre with serious literary traditions. The Campbell writers were nothing if not "solid," and many of them produced excellent work, but they were trapped in their own gestures, imprisoned by their success in creating an exuberant fandom. The new wave, by contrast, reached out toward everything that was outrageous and "hip" and pretended to laugh the old fandom out of existence. Like the writers of the *nouveau roman,* the new wave writers often attempted fiction that resembled an elaborate catalog of phenomenal reality, but just as often they dived boldly into the psyche's more obscure regions. The future, however, was rarely their focus.[21] Even though many new wave works have been dismissed as miscalculated and self-indulgent and condemned because they appear to result in reader alienation previously unknown in the field (as argued by Kingsley Amis in a well-known essay), the overarching result of this venture into new structures and stylistics has been the recognition of science fiction as an important element in postmodernism.[22] In the present literary climate, writers like J. G. Ballard and Philip K. Dick are perceived as having connections with Jorge Luis Borges and Italo Calvino, and one may argue that the long "exile" of the science fiction genre in the realm of pulp and pop culture is permanently over.[23]

Aldiss and Science Fiction's Coming of Age

Significantly, even as a matured science fiction genre was divorcing itself from its pulp origins, it was attaining respectability in academic circles. This respectability notably coincides with the period of the academic foundation of film studies and, perhaps ironically, with the reevaluation of other popular genres, which were newly sanctioned under the rubric of "camp" culture (that is, elite culture enjoying guilty pleasures and discovering powerful content in flimsy or subliterary forms). The analysis of science fiction, comics, radio, and film genres, among others, was eagerly taken up by a new academic industry that treated these as particularly revealing expressions of mass culture and used the sophisticated critical tools of postmodernism to expose their significant content, an activity that has played a further role in legitimizing popular forms.

Brian Aldiss's career is inextricably bound up with much of this literary history and with many of these cultural shifts of focus and value. Aldiss did not begin his career as a science fiction writer; yet after successfully entering the field, he published (in the 1970s and 1980s) a number of notable non-science fiction works. This fact divides him from most of the eminent science fiction writers of this century, who have been (by and large) unswerving in their devotion to the genre. On the other hand, Aldiss did not—at least early on—take the route of Kurt Vonnegut and use his relative success in "mainstream" writing to move away from science fiction entirely. In general, Aldiss has created a remarkably varied body of work in science fiction, exploring both the "extrapolative" and the "visionary" sides of the genre.[24] At the same time he has unself-consciously adopted a typically postmodern awareness of the "web of literature," since several of his works involve fictional extensions of science fiction or popular fiction classics, such as *Frankenstein, Dracula,* and *The Island of Doctor Moreau.* Aldiss (along with Philip José Farmer and several others) was also instrumental in going beyond the puritanical limitations that marred the treatment of sexual and scatological themes in the science fiction genre.[25] Aldiss has been a science fiction anthologist of major importance, a British equivalent to Judith Merril or Harlan Ellison. He has played a notable part at many science fiction conventions (these are, as noted above, a central part of the science fiction subculture) and has written a much admired (and much reprinted) history of science fiction.

In the light of these achievements, it is astonishing that Brian Aldiss is still a neglected writer, especially in North America. Most of his real peers—Philip K. Dick, James Blish, J. G. Ballard, Thomas Disch, Ursula K. Le Guin, and Stanislaw Lem—a few of these among the best writers of the era—are far better known. One can perhaps attribute Aldiss's comparative neglect to his versatility: versatility is dangerous in an era when writers are marketed by having their names associated with a single literary genre, subgenre, or series. In my view, however, versatility isn't the whole story. A deeper limitation may be Aldiss's failure to find a connected set of metaphors, a central textual world, an aesthetic thumbprint that would immediately identify his work as special and individual. If we think of writers as diverse as Franz Kafka, D. H. Lawrence, Virginia Woolf, Jorge Luis Borges, or Vladimir Nabokov, this point becomes clear. (To place it in the science fictional context, one might mention H. G. Wells, Philip K. Dick, or J. G. Ballard). All of the above-named artists created unique, unmistakable fictional worlds, one of the signal facts of their achievement, although this feat has been accomplished as well by many minor writers—Baron Corvo, G. K. Chesterton, and Henry Miller, to name a few—whose survival is more likely because of it. Thus, because of Wells's distinct aesthetic and textual world, Aldiss could (and did) parody him, just as any clever writer could parody Hemingway, whereas it would be impossible to parody the work of Brian Aldiss. From the perspective of the 1990s it is not difficult to see that Aldiss's commitment in the 1970s to the *nouveau roman* and to the post-Joycean novel, although it marked a courageous shift of focus and helped to enrich his later work, also involved a blurring of the contours of the Aldiss world. Also, this commitment probably came at just the wrong moment, engaging far too much of his productive energy when he was at the height of his creative power. Some of Aldiss's critics, notably Brian Griffin and David Wingrove, have tried to rescue Aldiss's work from its neglect by means of critical overkill.[26] Even a seriously deficient text such as *Frankenstein Unbound* is treated by these analysts as if it were as intellectually complex and as culturally significant as *The Crying of Lot Forty-Nine* or *Midnight's Children*. A much better procedure, I believe, is to admit that there are many failures in Aldiss's career and to attempt to locate the successes, in order to point to what is unique and most likely to endure among them.

The fact is that Brian Aldiss, prolific as he has been, has never written a single book widely recognized and acknowledged as touching upon a major tension point in modern culture. His books, of course, deal with most of the major intellectual issues of the age: the cold war and the underlying rivalry between capitalism and communism; the threat of nuclear war; the possibility of ecological disaster; the fate of humanism in a world that is becoming increasingly mechanized and soulless; the question of communication in an increasingly fragmented society. Yet Aldiss never crystallized his vision of east-west rivalry in a single compelling metaphor of ideological entropy, as Orwell did in *1984*. He was not as consistently trenchant about the dystopian smothering of the individual as was Philip K. Dick in his best novels, nor did he match Dick's superb achievement in the vein of alternate history, *The Man in the High Castle*. He did not dramatize ecological disaster as potently as did John Christopher in *No Blade of Grass* or John Brunner in *Stand on Zanzibar*, or in a manner that seized the popular imagination, as did John Wyndham in *The Day of the Triffids*. He did not render the terrors

of the nuclear age as an aspect of the terror of history itself as Walter
Miller Jr. memorably did in *A Canticle for Leibowitz.* He did not capture
in a single famous opus the human-machine conundrum as did Karel
Čapek or Arthur C. Clarke or even Isaac Asimov. He did not treat the
post-Wellsian invasion from space theme in the startlingly original manner of Clarke's *Childhood's End.* He has never quite matched Olaf Stapledon's fame as an epic chronicler of human and extrahuman civilization.
Aldiss is less known than he should be for his probing of the epistemological and communication questions raised by the possibility of
extraterrestrial societies, simply because in no single work did he equal
the metaphorical ingenuity visible in Stanislaw Lem's *Solaris* or Clarke's
Rendezvous with Rama.

All of this is true, yet Aldiss is a far better writer of fiction than Asimov, a far more multifarious literary talent than Clarke, and a much
more prolific and complex writer than Walter Miller. He has shown a
more varied grasp of the human condition than Christopher or Brunner,
has plied his gifts with a lighter, defter hand by far than either Stapledon or Aldiss's own contemporary J. G. Ballard. In fact, no writer
except Ballard, and possibly Vonnegut, has been able to excel both as a
science fiction writer and as a serious mainstream novelist to the extent
that Aldiss has. When Anthony Burgess listed Aldiss's *Life in the West* as
one of the 99 best postwar British novels it was not merely the tribute of
one somewhat neglected talent to another but a genuine recognition of
the depth and timeliness of a book that, despite its limitations, almost
reaches the first level of fictional achievement.

What follows is an attempt to reevaluate Brian Aldiss's work, not in
order to pay compliments to his intelligence or versatility (for he needs
none), but in order to single out the Aldiss fiction that is likely to survive to become part of the literary history of our time. In this world of
transformed media and shifting canons, it would be foolish to suggest
that one's conclusions as to what part of a writer's work may endure and
under what rubric could be more than a guess. To make a start, however, at separating what is most valuable from what is merely interesting, puts the guesswork on some kind of footing, however slippery. It is
my hope that not only science fiction fans, but also the general reader
and in particular those who make decisions about what fiction is worth
republishing, will be stimulated by these pages to get in touch with, to
reconsider, and to reprint some excellent Brian Aldiss texts. The rest will
be up to those unknown, mysterious, and much-written-about pres-
ences who make all the final decisions about literary matters, as indeed
about everything: the inhabitants of the future.

Chapter Two

The Mainstream
Science Fiction Novels

We devotees of SF enjoy its diversity of opinion, the bustle of bright and dark, the
clash of progress and entropy, the clamour of theories about the past, the future, the
ever-present present, everything.
We doubt: therefore we are.

—Brian Aldiss, *The Detached Retina* (1995)

Non-Stop

Brian Aldiss began his career as a science fiction writer with short fiction, but unlike many excellent science fiction practitioners, he did not derive his first novel, *Non-Stop,* from his very first stories. *Non-Stop* appeared in 1958 with Faber & Faber (published in the United States as *Starship,* 1959) and was successful enough to enable Aldiss to take up a career as a full-time professional writer.

Non-Stop is a generational spaceship story, with a well-conceived plot whose effectiveness is only partially undermined by the giveaway North American title. Some elements in the book are original and are what we think of as typical Brian Aldiss, while others borrow much from the common run of 1950s science fiction, in particular from the work of Robert Heinlein.[1] The protagonist Roy Complain, for example, is a no-nonsense man of action, battling his way through deceit and complexity and showing an effectiveness directly related to his capacity for violence and for making decisions on the spur of the moment.

Roy Complain lives in what seems to be an underground world, in a tribal society that Aldiss evokes in convincing detail. We learn that certain of the tribes migrate, establishing frontiers that change over time, although only slightly. At the territorial boundaries lie "wild" areas, where pigs and other creatures roam among "ponics" or weedy plants growing under artificial illumination. The tribes have some minimal technology, for example, stun guns or dazers, and each group is struc-

11

tured in a loose hierarchy with the chieftain, his cronies, hunters, and guards near the top. Complain's group possesses a kind of scripture encompassing moral rules and advice, but their conduct is even more affected by the existence of "ghosts" or "giants" (who mysteriously appear and disappear and who resemble ordinary humans), and by mutants and colonies of super-clever rats. It turns out, and not incidentally, that Complain's tribal group, known as the "Dizzies" are all very short in stature, well under six feet.

The life of these tribes seems to be quite restricted and brutish, so it is hardly surprising that when Complain's wife is kidnapped and possibly murdered, he agrees to join a group of four others who will go on a quest to seek a better one. As the novel unfolds we are carefully led to a major revelation—that the tribal "underground" is an artificial environment; Complain and the others are in fact trapped on a giant spaceship, which, as we learn later, is called Big Dog.

The explorers, probing their environment, find that main corridor passageways are blocked, creating separate sealed units, which they have to circumvent by using side passages. In the course of their passage they go through an area of weightlessness; they meet some of the "giants" (who turn out to be ordinary-sized men, a starship crew of the Star Trek variety, really). At one point Complain is shot with a stun gun by these nonvicious humans and, while immobile, he undergoes a strange ritual, one conducted by some intelligent rats who use a caged rabbit to communicate telepathically with him! This event takes place near the ship's swimming pool, and Aldiss turns the whole sequence into a successful exercise in estrangement from the familiar so characteristic of science fiction.

As the explorers advance, one of their number, Wantage, runs amuck and is killed by a roving group of maverick Dizzies from the ship's forequarters or Forwards; the others are captured. The third, or "Forwards" section brings us close to conventional and coy science fiction romance as Complain meets Vyann, an attractive woman who is a lieutenant among the Forwards crew. Coincidences begin to pile up. Complain's brother Gregg is part of a marauding gang. When Complain and Vyann go to negotiate with him, they learn that the rats on board ship are well-organized and vicious; they are capturing the other animals and threaten to take over the ship. Gregg gives his brother's party a blow-torch, and the group breaks into the control room. Here the explorers experience a first vision of space—a scene that Aldiss seems to underplay. They also learn that the controls have been destroyed—which means they still lack power over the fate of the ship.

The root of their predicament is now gradually revealed. Big Dog had originally been sent to settle a planet of the Procyon ("Little Dog") star group. On the return trip, a fault in the water supply brought on a kind of epidemic that decimated the crew (and probably the colony). The ship's captain was Complain, ancestor of Aldiss's protagonist. We learn that by generation count they should already have reached earth, but something seems to be wrong: they fear they may have shot past it. In fact, Big Dog has been orbiting earth for several generations and during that time has been under observation from the home planet. The ghosts and giants known to the Dizzies are actually earth-sent investigators and manipulators; their job is to keep the various societies on the ship stable. Meanwhile, on earth, scientists are working to try to find a way to change the metabolism of the Dizzies. The fact is that the Dizzies cannot be easily transferred to earth, simply because they have mutated and are not only smaller in stature but, due to the artificial day-night on ship, have a different metabolic rate. (They are called Dizzies because they live at four times the speed of the humans.) They have a life expectancy of only twenty earth years.

As the story concludes, a pitched battle between the Dizzies and the giants takes place, and the ship is wrecked and flies apart, although each part seems to be space-worthy. The rats roam around, terrifying everyone, using moths as their scouts. Complain becomes even more of a comic book hero in this section. He forces the truth out of an earth spy and compels the radio message to earth that will bring the longed-for rescue.

This story has excellent momentum and shows great confidence in the telling.[2] Aldiss creates the world of the starship effectively, and throughout the writing is strong and simple, although never poetic or visionary. We follow the action through Complain, a quite simple man groping to understand his world and well aware that he is unhappy in it, but the emotions of most of the other characters are also recognizably human and the interactions of the various groups reasonably credible. The unfortunate title change in the American edition and the overinformative blurbs on the book cover tend to undermine the skill with which Aldiss controls the reader's awareness of just what kind of world Complain inhabits and make Complain's uncertainty about whether indeed he is on a spaceship seem more stupid than would otherwise be the case.[3]

Aldiss's first science fiction novel is not only a generational spaceship story; it is also a "false reality" story—another familiar science fiction structure.[4] We are slowly made aware of the first reality—the spaceship—only to find there is another reality: the spaceship is under watch and is in fact orbiting the earth. Spies among the Dizzies report back to the controllers: the alienation effect is multiplied. Aldiss, writing in the fifties, the decade of the catastrophe story, prefers to portray the cold war as a playing out of paranoia. The spaceship Little Dog is a metaphor for a social entity where uncertainty is the norm and betrayal a fact of life.[5] The benevolent earth programmers remind us that even those "on our side" do not really give us what we want. The Dizzies are left to continue their journey in ignorance, to circle earth without ever getting there, surrounded by deception and subject to constant manipulation. While this kind of story may indeed have been promoted by the east-west confrontations of the cold war, the theme is much broader; it carries on and extends the Wells idea that our planet itself might be under watch. Cultural paranoia? Not exactly: the post-Darwinian sense of the cosmic reach of life and evolution, the vast extension of time, made the invasion-of-earth motif more than a metaphor for a specific social insecurity, more than an odd collective mania.[6] Darwinism not only chastened humanity's idea of itself but made human uniqueness seem improbable: the whole cosmos might well be inhabited by intelligent life, and, despite C. S. Lewis's notable attempt to assert the reverse, aliens might very likely be enemies.[7] This theme has huge possibilities for extension and many levels of realization: its intriguing but simple-minded presentation in the 1959 movie, *The Thing,* may be compared with the complexity of the epistemologically uncertain abduction stories of the nineties, with their hints of an earth randomly subject to intervention and experiment by less-than-benevolent visitors.[8]

Aldiss refuses to follow that kind of script all the way. He inverts the alien-human confrontation by turning humans into aliens who haunt the very human Dizzies. Such an upside-down world could easily lead to madness, or at least to neurotic paralysis, but Aldiss seizes upon the Heinlein solution: take action. Ruled by common sense, strong fists or a handy laser, the Edgar Rice Burroughs or Robert Heinlein hero could deal with these problems. "To hell with theories. Stow that brotherly love; let's blast our way out of here!"—a too-simple solution to a complex metaphor of entrapment and one with an uncertain morality. In the Big Dog world, murder seems acceptable, violence is part of life.[9]

Roy Complain is angry, a man breaking out of repression: he has been conditioned by the tribal gospel and the pseudo-Freudian programming and is just waking up. But Aldiss doesn't achieve the complexity of his overall structural conception in his hero or in the writing—the usual problem in this kind of Campbell-derived science fiction.[10] Some of the dialogue is wooden and a few characters are inconsistent. For example, Aldiss seems uncertain whether to present Marapper, the preacher, as a real scoundrel or a lovable and lucky, though conniving, eccentric. As far as the total effect is concerned, the unveiling of the truth in such stories often leaves the reader with the feeling he or she gets from a good crossword puzzle or an Agatha Christie mystery: the intellectual sorting out is satisfactory, or nearly so, but the superficiality of the characters undermines the strength of the structure, so that many readers will fail to find a psychological or social truth that startles and leads toward a deeper perception of reality. No mature reader could really care what happens to Roy Complain; he is just the focal point of our dawning knowledge of what kind of story this is and what its metaphorical reach conveys.

If *Non-Stop* owes much to the Heinlein tradition, it also derives directly from Wells and from the catastrophe novels of the fifties. As in *The Time Machine* and *The Island of Doctor Moreau,* we have the notion of innocent life being exploited by scientific manipulation. Behind the disaster on Big Dog lies the pollution of the water supply, and the out-of-control rats signify a kind of natural revenge for humankind's bungled interventions in nature. Anxiety about class figures here too, and Aldiss's specific perceptions seem to refer to the British postwar welfare state, where, it seems, help is always present but often maddeningly irrelevant to the real needs of the helpless. In this situation, religion is powerless, a half-sham, as it usually turns out to be in the fifties novels of ecological breakdown and in the fiction and films of the Angry Young Men, the redbrick intellectuals with whom Aldiss has much in common.

Non-Stop proved that Brian Aldiss had a gift for plot-making, that he was a writer capable of integrating ideas and techniques derived from a wide diversity of sources, and that he had a genuine and creative sense of the multiple possibilities of science fiction. Yet, though it is much more than merely a lively and likable period piece, the novel strikes the reader today as a work that offers only a glimpse of the exciting developments that were to come in the fiction of Brian Aldiss in the next two decades.

Hothouse

At the beginning of the 1960s, seeking new markets and contact with the American scene, Aldiss published two minor novels in New York, *Bow Down to Nul* (1960, with Ace Books; published in Britain as *The Interpreter* in 1961) and *The Primal Urge* (1961, with Ballantine). The first of these is a comic version of the alien contact novel, a hastily written and pointless book, while the second is one of those jejune sex-fantasies that would plague the whole decade of "liberation." Meanwhile, Aldiss was working on one of his best and most original fictions, one that would give a completely new dimension to the environmental concerns of the science fiction writers of the fifties.

Published in 1962, *Hothouse* (published in the United States in an abridged version as *The Long Afternoon of Earth,* also 1962) is a powerful fantasy only minimally grounded in accepted scientific ideas. The novel describes an earth of the far future, one that has been blasted and changed by a sun that is only some few generations from becoming a nova. The inevitable fate of earth is to be wiped out in the forthcoming holocaust; nonetheless, although the relation of plant to animal forms has been radically altered by the sun's transformation, life is still luxuriant, still evolving. While one half of earth has become a tropical jungle of daunting depth and complexity, the other half is an impenetrable and forbidding darkness, a cold region where the sun never shines. We are initially introduced to the jungle region and its teeming plant life, dominated by a single immense banyan tree, but the narrative later carries us along part of the shoreline of the great sea and also makes a strange (and rather unconvincing) diversion to the moon.

Although animal life occupies only a small niche in the *Hothouse* world, Aldiss concentrates on human fate, following the lives of some members of a tribe of tree-dwellers descended from present-day Homo sapiens. In the *Hothouse* world humans live in the middle branches of the great world-tree: the dark undergrowth, the forest floor, is alien to them, while the treetops, difficult to reach, are the scene of tribal rituals involving changes of leadership and migration. The human tribes are insignificant and rather powerless; they lack technology and their intelligence has become specialized and inadequate to promote improvements. At the same time, terrors surround them; formerly harmless plants have adapted well and evolved into some terrifying forms. Competition for survival is everywhere fierce.

Although the reader may feel that in *Hothouse* Aldiss sometimes comes close to being carried away by his own exuberant imagination, one of the book's strengths is clearly the descriptive writing, which is imaginative and functional.[11] Aldiss convincingly creates strange and thoroughly intriguing variations of animal, and especially of vegetable, life. The oddest hybrids appear and names pour forth, risking silliness, yet never undermining the narrative thrust. In the end, we find ourselves as involved with the characters that inhabit this future earth as we are with Lewis Carroll's Mad Hatter and White Rabbit.

From the very beginning Aldiss is adept at moving the narrative along, even while creating the sense of a fantastically beautiful and dangerous world:

> The women climbed slowly now, alert as the odd tigerfly zoomed in their direction. Splashes of colour grew everywhere, attached to the tree, hanging from lines, or drifting free. Lianas and fungi blossomed. Dumblers moved mournfully through the tangle. As they gained height, the air grew fresher and colour rioted, azures and crimsons, yellows and mauves, all the beautifully tinted snares of nature.
>
> A dripperlip sent its scarlet dribbles of gum down the trunk. Several thinpins, with vegetable skill, stalked the drops, pounced, and died. Lily-yo and Flor went by on the other side.[12]

Lily-yo, the head of this dauntless band of humans, decides it is time to perform a ritual called "going up." After some difficulties, she and another float into space, with the aid of a giant traverser spider-plant. Protected from harmful radiation, they reach the moon, where fellow humans meet them. Among these moon-dwellers a plan is afoot to go back down and conquer the earth, and the newcomers are enlisted to join.

The humans left on earth must fend for themselves. Toy is the band's chief, but she leads them into some trouble, and the independent-minded Gren soon breaks away from the group. Gren finds himself alone at the terrible boundary of sea and jungle. He is reunited with the others, but he leaves again, this time joined by Poyly, one of the women. An intelligent morel attaches itself to his skull and guides him through most of the rest of the adventures. The morel is both a blessing and a curse, but initially it helps him survive. Poyly and Gren capture a girl named Yattmur who is a member of another tribe known as the fisher folk. They meet strange creatures known as the tummy-bellies, who are umbilically connected to a mother tree, although capable, as it turns out, of moving freely as well. The tummy-bellies, as we soon see, are the comic relief of the story, and Aldiss uses them lovingly, creating an amusing and convincing speech-style for them and bringing off some of his funniest verbal effects.

> You can see we four sad sufferers are fatally dying of the death that comes to all green and pink things, so you tell us to stand up, because to make any standing position will kill us badly, so that you kick us when our souls are gone and we can only be dead at you and not crying with our harmless mouths. O we fall down from our lying flat at such a sly idea, great herder! (*Hothouse,* 141)

The story, however, keeps its serious focus. Poyly is killed when the tummy-bellies are cut away from the nurturing tree. Gren and Yattmur mate and eventually have a child. At one point nearly caught by a devouring volcano, at another nearly swallowed by a deceptive cave mist, Gren and his companions land on an island. They encounter, among other things, a weird advertising balloon that comically spouts election slogans and is finally downed by hungry birds. They float to land on migrating stalker plants and arrive at a mountainous region on the boundary of sun and darkness where they meet the so-called "sharp-fur" people. These bearlike and dangerous long-tailed mammals intrigue the tummy-belly men. (Unfortunately the latter eventually become their victims). The crisis occurs when the morel wants to fasten to Gren and Yattmur's baby. The arrival of an intelligent fishlike land creature, the Sodal Ye, carried by a symbiotic slave and attended by women who can time-travel and spy out the path just ahead, changes things. From the Sodal Ye Yattmur learns how to free Gren from the morel. She traps it in a gourd; later it fastens itself to the Sodal Ye. A traverser falls to earth and on it are Lily-yo and some of the others. But by now the morel has combined its intelligence with that of the Sodal Ye and tells the humans exactly how the universe has unfolded and will unfold. Spores are carried from one system to another. Life begins in simple forms, evolves; conditions change; devolution takes place. Everything is crushed into simple forms again and life floats away to yet another system. So life continues seemingly forever, in endless cycles.

Now a parting takes place. Hearing that earth is doomed, Lily-yo and the others float away on the traverser in search of a new home. Gren and Yattmur, however, choose to remain on earth. They know they can survive there through several generations, and they explain that such a prospect is preferable to being trapped in the gut of a vegetable in space. Thus the novel ends without tragedy, and although the fate of the humans left on earth seems rather bleak, the overall mood is very positive.

Although parts of it had appeared as separate Hugo-winning stories, *Hothouse* proved to be a controversial novel; some science fiction writers disliked it or turned against it on the grounds that it was clearly not science fiction at all but rather fantasy. Kingsley Amis and others, however, praised the novel for its imaginative richness.[13] Richard Matthews compares the story to *The Odyssey*, which seems wide of the mark, although he has many useful things to say about the grounding of the story in myth.[14] The earth of *Hothouse* has become a dangerous Eden, dominated by a world tree, divided into dark and light, a world in which instinct and intelligence both appear necessary for survival. This future earth is also primeval, a hallucinatory realm in which the wildest mystical flights are possible but where a small mistake can easily erase a life.

While this environment naturally makes heroes and heroism unlikely (Odysseus's world is, by comparison, almost a playground), Aldiss does find ways of generating sympathy in the reader: Poyly's death is a shock and Gren's escape from the dominance of the morel is a relief, despite the usefulness of the morelian insights. The humor works extremely well, neither undermining our sense of constant danger nor diminishing the power of such events as Gren's unitive vision in the cave. Throughout, Aldiss shifts perspectives with great skill, moving between Gren and Yattmur and balancing individual portrayals with evocations of the various species.

Hothouse is an extrapolative fantasy, one that remains well within the bounds of science fiction, although emphasizing the creation of a fantastic world rather than foregrounding the mythos or structure of the story itself.[15] In Aldiss's novel the story is in fact virtually consumed by the world, one reason the book bears little resemblance to *The Odyssey*. *Hothouse* is extrapolative because it clearly derives from an actual or possible earth, one whose radical climate changes create the new "topos," or setting, and that setting is so extreme as to generate the estrangement from our known world that is fundamental to science fiction.[16] While incidental episodes of *Hothouse* evoke strong fantasy or mythical connections (the tummy-bellies, the traversers, the Sodal Ye, the banyan tree), the controlling setting clearly makes the book science fiction. (*Alice in Wonderland,* on the other hand, could not be science fiction because one can imagine no world extrapolated or projected from ours into which its mythos would comfortably fit). The fact that such a brilliant and innovative book led critics to raise the issue of genre, however, is significant, for this was only an early stage in the evolution of Aldiss's boundary-stretching art. Despite his obvious talents, he was to go on in the next few years to innovations that would bounce him straight out of the affections of many die-hard science fiction fans, without necessarily gaining him the full attention of the mainstream or avant-garde critics.

Greybeard

In 1964 Aldiss published a major postcatastrophe novel, *Greybeard.* This book not only reflects his kinship with other writers of the era who were exploring the possible consequences of nuclear testing; it represents as well an early attempt by Aldiss to create a double narrative structure in which present and past are continually juxtaposed, slowing the narrative momentum, but in the end enriching the reader's perspective on the characters. Although this technique works quite well in *Greybeard* it is even more effectively used in Aldiss's later mainstream novels, in *Forgotten Life,* in particular.

Greybeard opens in the year 2029 in a small village settlement in southern England, a place called Sparcot, to the west of Oxford. War and a devastating nuclear accident have decimated the human population and made most of the survivors (although not all higher animals) sterile. An aging humanity has sunk back into a kind of careless semibarbarism, which has both comical and pathetic aspects. Sparcot is ruled by a "boss" named Jim Mole who believes in first-strike aggression and survival of the fittest, although the 70- and 80-year-olds he marshals to exact "tribute" from helpless travelers and to defend the village against small bands of human and animal encroachers appear ludicrously inadequate for the job.

Algernon Timberlane, a "younger" man in his fifties who is known as Greybeard, decides to leave the settlement. With his wife Martha, and a few loyal friends, he sails down the Thames toward Oxford and London. In the course of this trip through what is a kind of overgrown and dangerous wasteland, the past is filled in for us. We learn about the wars of the late twentieth century, the subsequent epidemics that resulted in the breakdown of law and order, and also about Timberlane's childhood. His father and mother, already estranged by her love for another man, were further divided by Timberlane senior's failure in business: a manufacturer of children's toys, he finds the market for these toys failing all over the world. This market collapse occurs because nuclear testing in space has disrupted the Van Allen belt and has showered the earth with radiation.[17] Worldwide sterility results; no more children are being born and toys are not required. A small effect, it seems, but it devastates

Greybeard's childhood because, confronted by loss on all sides, his father commits suicide.

In the chaos that marked the beginning of the twenty-first century, Greybeard had joined an international group known by its acronym as DOUCH(E), meaning Documentation of Universal Contemporary History, English Branch. The purpose of this group was to monitor a world situation in which the human race itself was threatened with extinction. DOUCH(E) was rather powerless, however, against the increasing social chaos. Timberlane and his wife barely manage to survive their experiences in Washington, D.C. (where she is kidnapped by a lunatic entertainer), and in Oxford, where they are both sentenced to be executed by the local warlord, Croucher. After 11 years in Sparcot, Greybeard and Martha, along with Jeff Pitt and Charley Samuels—fellow-villagers who had shared some of their past—and a few others, venture into the outside world.

They travel downriver and encounter the dead and dying, thieves, mountebanks, and a rabble of ancient survivors, notably a spurious medicine man named Bunny Jingdangelow, who claims to be able to make people live forever. They arrive in Oxford and discover the city to be half-ruined and flooded with a few effete and cynical dons in charge at Christ Church College. Greybeard finds a vehicle he had once driven; he longs to buy it back, but cannot earn the money to do so. He and Martha push on toward London and the great sea. They never quite reach it: however, on the way they again encounter Bunny Jingdangelow and his entourage; he is now "the Master," a religious fraud who promises the naive the gift of eternal life in exchange for food and money. He has also acquired a beautiful young female companion, a situation that stirs up some conflict between Greybeard and Martha, the latter once again frustrated by her own lack of children and understandably envious of this image of potentially fecund life she sees in the Master's bed. Yet to the surprise of Greybeard and Martha, the Master approaches them, and, claiming to have grown tired of his own deceptions, offers to give up his charades and his followers and to travel on with them. They reject him, but then save him from a few grotesquely misshapen young people who have emerged from the forest to attack him in the night. It now becomes clear that "gnomes and elves" rumored to have reappeared in the countryside must be such young people, who, fearing for their lives among the desperate older folk, have "gone wild" in the overgrown wilderness that is England. When Greybeard shoots and wounds one of the Master's attackers, a young boy,

Martha immediately takes on the role of healer and mother, and the novel ends with this image of a new connection between the generations that may have large significance for the future of the human species.

Knowledgeable readers of *Greybeard* will immediately place it within a long tradition of texts recounting catastrophes and the end of civilization. Byron's "Darkness" and Mary Shelley's *The Last Man,* Victorian popular novels such as Shiel's *The Purple Cloud, After London* by Richard Jefferies, and *The War of the Worlds* by Wells provided examples that the science fiction writers of the fifties and sixties, in particular, could draw upon in order to exorcise fears generated by the cold war and the nuclear arms race. In many respects the ironic inversions of both natural and social life in *Greybeard* resemble those of John Wyndham's *The Day of the Triffids* and John Christopher's *No Blade of Grass,* while certain characters could easily move from any one of these texts to another. All three novels assume the possibility of a world-scale catastrophe that will turn society upside-down. All assume that governments will be unable to deal with any such crisis and that the rule of law will not survive. All three center on a quest through what might well be called "the man-made wasteland of the world" for something better. The assumption of all these writers is that the values of a "decent" and practical individualism can survive, even in such a brutalized and primitive future. The large influence behind all of these works is *The War of the Worlds,* but Aldiss seems in addition to have recalled a few scenes from the 1936 Wells movie *Things to Come.* (Croucher very much resembles the warlord played by Ralph Richardson in that ponderous but intriguing film). Although *Greybeard* is a book of its time, the enduring popularity of this theme of catastrophe and its accompanying imagery of social breakdown is testified to by the relatively recent "Mad Max" movie trilogy from Australia.

To the informed reader, then, *Greybeard* may seem like merely one more variation on an overfamiliar theme, and Aldiss's attempt to give it depth and resonance by juxtaposing the present with the past may end up being a distraction, although it clearly extends the range of the book in various ways. Greybeard himself, sensitive and cautious, is a rather lackluster protagonist, although a welcome departure from the Roy Complain species of man of action. The Englishness of the characters, their often grotesque appearances, odd costumes and beliefs, their eccentricities, and mostly harmless foolishness—these characteristics enable us to relate this book not only to Aldiss's first novel, *The Bright-fount Diaries,* and to his nearly contemporary short novel, *The Saliva Tree,* but to the long tradition—extending from Shakespeare to Dickens, Wells, and Hardy—of depicting yokels, "mechanics," small shopkeepers, and incorrigible individualists from the working classes in a manner that is both affectionate and (in some cases) condescending. Aldiss, who is objective and who does not condescend, confirms his link to this honorable tradition in many ways, not the least of which is by his skill at finding colorful names for his motley characters. Besides Algernon Timberlane and the others already mentioned, the novel introduces us to Sam Bulstow, Towin Thomas, the man known as Norsgrey who has a badger for a wife, Bunny Jingdangelow, Joseph Flitch, and a few others who would not be out of place in Hardy's Wessex.[18]

Despite its derivative nature (even the quite satisfying ending of Aldiss's book owes something to William Golding's *The Inheritors*), *Greybeard* is a skillfully wrought novel. Its sober and rather matter-of-fact style lends conviction to the fantastic world depicted, while the natural setting is rendered with unerring skill. The characters, as indicated, range from the wildest grotesques to the rather solid Greybeard and Martha, the latter couple emerging with considerable strength despite their incorrigible homeyness, their somewhat overcozy dialogue, and the frustrating uneventfulness of their journey. *Greybeard* certainly has its faults—lack of narrative momentum and the failure of Aldiss's invention to take him very far past his models—but the image that remains in the reader's mind is a reassuring one, that of an intelligent couple maintaining a loving and creative relationship through social and natural crises that threaten to destroy everything humanity has built. This image is surprisingly traditional, yet it is one that Aldiss confidently sets against the delusions and chicaneries that inevitably result from the breakdown of a world that has gone too far in the worship of mechanism and political expediency.

Two Minor Novels of the 1960s

The Dark Light Years (1964) is, by contrast, a much more limited success as a novel, although outrageous and provocative in its thematic focus. It tells of the encounter between humanity and a race of distastefully natured alien creatures who prefer to live surrounded by their own waste. Alternating points of view are employed to give the perspectives of both sides: the basic irony is that while the alien Utods have much wisdom to share with humankind, they have never developed a shame or taboo code in relation to their excreta; the humans, on the other hand, have their own forms of self-pollution, more subtle, but perhaps equally distasteful. Toward the end of the novel the human director of the Exozoo in which the Utods are confined, approaches them on their own terms, defecating on the plastic floor of their cage. Eventually, the earth is destroyed, the last of the humans depart and the captive Utods, whose planet has also been decimated, look forward to the prospect of freedom.

What is really conveyed in the novel—and this idea is why Aldiss creates the Utods as they are—is the somber thought that human civilization, too, is both literally and figuratively a prisoner of its own cloacal necessities. A complex and beautiful machine, a Rembrandt, a fugue of Bach—the "custom and ceremony" of civilization celebrated by W. B. Yeats—all these occupy the apex of a pyramid, the base of which rests in muck and is surrounded by a scream.[19] Through sublimation and repression, by putting things out of sight, we save our sensibilities and make the "higher life" possible. It is the job of the science fiction writer, Aldiss seems to say, to take away the blinders. The Swiftian vision implicit in *The Dark Light Years* is not fully realized, however, because the writing does not follow through relentlessly enough on the book's premise. Humor, which is a gentle mocking art, and which Aldiss employs throughout, is incompatible with the necessities of the sardonic. When Swift writes: "Last night I saw a woman flayed, and you would hardly believe how much it altered her person for the worse," or when William Blake advises: "Sooner murder an infant in its cradle than nurse unacted desires," we are very close to the bone, very much in the presence of nearly intolerable insights about the human condition. Aldiss falls short of this and disperses too much of the potential of his "savage indignation" in mere amusement, twisting away from the main vision to suggest a self-conscious dig at the science fiction genre itself. As a result *The Dark-Light Years* is more of a curiosity than a major work.

Earthworks (1965) suffers from a similar problem, although it lacks a comparable ingenuity. The main character Knowle Nowland, who tells the story, is one of the large species of tight-lipped, grimly enduring science fiction heroes. He roams about a bleak, polluted, overpopulated world like some decontextualized James Bond in search of a Dr. No or a Goldfinger, the villain responsible for the catastrophe Noland experiences. In this world, however, the villain is humanity itself, and the earth—with its horrible platform cities, labor camps, and bleak landscapes—cannot possibly be saved by more violence—is, in fact, not worth saving, given the range of human experience Noland and the other characters seem capable of. *Earthworks,* in short, creates a Philip K. Dick or Pohl and Kornbluth-like dystopia but fails to redeem it with the humanity of the former or with the "bounce" or humor of the latter. The bankruptcy of imagination visible here, the uncertainty of tone (unaccountably, humor obtrudes without relieving the bleakness) suggest that Aldiss had reached a dead end in his mainstream science fiction storytelling.

It is hardly surprising, then, that the latter part of the 1960s, coinciding with many of the excitements of the new wave, saw Aldiss publish a series of highly experimental novels, books that nearly served to lead him away from science fiction entirely (see chapter 4). Or that in the early 1970s he brought out *Billion Year Spree,* giving his own perspective on the history of science fiction, a marvelous study but one that unfortunately did not reconcile many dyed-in-the-wool science fiction readers to his increasingly erratic development as a fiction-writer (see chapter 6).

The Malacia Tapestry

In 1976, finally, came *The Malacia Tapestry,* a long and lovingly detailed novel of speculative fiction and a work that obviously aims for great complexity of plot and elegance of style. The book featured Aldiss-chosen illustrations by the eighteenth-century Venetian artist Tiepolo, which add to the general air of sophistication surrounding the text, although the effect of these illustrations was somewhat undermined by the garish pulp covers on both the British and American paperback editions.[20] Yet despite its pretensions, its promise of rococo elegance or Byzantine complexity of style, mood, and theme, the book received a mixed reception from reviewers, and in retrospect it is not difficult to see why.

The Malacia Tapestry takes place in a kind of alternative-world Venice of the Renaissance-baroque-rococo period, a self-contained and colorful yet decadent city-state. The city is ruled by a supreme council, and dissent is dangerous; Bosnian Ottoman enemies are at the gates. Even so, the life of pleasure seems to continue unthreatened. We soon learn that however much this city resembles the historical Venice, it is radically different. There are, for example, "flighted people," who are like the Malacians except that they have wings and can fly; there are also various reptilian forms, some small and harmless by nature, others, in the surrounding forests, more dangerous. Malacia is in fact not Venice at all, but a Venice in an alternative world, one in which the reptiles are the ancestors of the dominant forms, including even the humans. In the Malacian world evolution functioned differently, while the historical Renaissance has been deprived of its role as intellectual catalyst. Thus, though the characters in Aldiss's novel are very similar—too similar—to those in the 1950s style Frank Yerby or Samuel Shellabarger historical fiction, this book departs from the genre of historical novel in at least one respect, for Malacia has not entered history as we know it. It is a place mummified by its own richly embroidered patterns, more like a tapestry or a decorative panel than a dynamic social entity.[21]

The story is narrated by the main character, Perian de Chirolo, an impecunious actor, a young man-about-town, who lives by his wits and pursues the ladies. He and his close friend Guy de Lambant connect throughout the story and eventually become rivals. A traveling magician named Bengtsohn arrives in the city; he has invented a machine called a zahnoscope, something like a still camera that takes slide pictures of theatrical scenarios, one of which Perian performs in. The machine seems harmless enough, yet change is threatening to this society and the authorities in the end destroy the machine and murder its inventor.

The first part of the book deals mostly with Perian's amorous adventures. He has a lusty encounter with his impresario's mistress, La Singla, and attempts to seduce a poor girl named Letitia; later, he is successful with her, as indeed he is with a rich young woman, Armida, and also with Bedalar, de Lambant's chosen woman. Perian soon becomes something of a civic hero, riding a balloon over the besieging Ottoman forces. Other balloons drop plague-ridden corpses on the Turks and the siege is lifted. Armida, whose father disapproves of Perian, has been spirited away to the forest region of Juracia. She manages to get Perian invited there to a hunt, for in Juracia the forest is full of the old saurian beasts, the most dangerous of which are the huge "tyrant-greaves" and the menacing "devil-jaws." In the woods, Perian has a vision and comes under a kind of evil spell. He ruminates on the meaning of this vision, reflecting that he hasn't broken his vow to Armida, except perhaps a little with Letitia, the poor girl. This reflection seems strange in view of his cavortings with Bedalar; are we to believe Perian is this naive, or is it an authorial slip? At the end of book 2 Perian has another forest vision, one in which he sees certain ancient spirits, the embodiments of the so-called "natural religion" of Malacia. These spirits are engaged in capturing a woman named Theodora, a reincarnation of the ancient empress. From them Perian receives a kind of half-frightening promise of mature enlightenment and is granted a wish. He asks to be allowed to save Armida. Shortly afterward, he surprises Armida and de Lambant making love on a forest path and does indeed save her, by killing one of the forest beasts, a "devil-jaw," which attacks the group and wounds him.

In book 3 Perian rests and recovers from his wounds. The relationship with Armida is still uncertain. Perian visits Nicholas Fatember, a fresco artist, and they discuss reality and illusion, art and worldly success. Fatember suggests to Perian that there are many "realities," and that art which tries to mimic what appears to be reality is limited. (Is this meant to nudge the reader into a sense of what all these doings in Malacia are about?) Perian meanwhile begins to be disturbed by de Lambant's attentions to Armida; he seems to have forgotten that he himself has slept with de Lambant's woman, Bedalar. Aldiss's rather one-dimensional protagonist here sounds increasingly old-womanish and self-pitying. (In this section the narrative seems to be marking time.) Things do come to a climax, however, as Perian attends his sister's wedding and is rejected by Armida's father, de Hoytola, who tells him to quit the scene, hinting darkly about Bengtsohn's fate. Armida by this time has become de Lambant's mistress. When Perian discovers this turn of events he attacks his friend and is promptly thrown out of the castle. His connection with Bedalar (which he, or Aldiss, seemed to have forgotten) is now brought up against him. After the shock of Bengtsohn's death (Perian sees his head floating in a canal), our hero is comforted by La Singla, the impresario's mistress, who has suddenly become a model of sensual and worldly wisdom. Perian remains superficial and unfocused; as the long novel ends, the reader may decide that the protagonist, although much chastened, is hardly a much wiser (or more interesting) man.

The style of *The Malacia Tapestry* is fluid and entertaining, perhaps dangerously so, yet the narrative lacks direction.[22] Aldiss's plot is of a fantastic complexity, but the characters are not deeply or convincingly rendered. Perian de Chirolo, in particular, is hard to keep in focus. Most of the time he is frivolous and fickle-minded, a fact that makes his intense love for Armida hard to accept. One can understand Perian wanting to go to bed with her; or to marry her for her money—but his romantic obsession with her will be incomprehensible to most readers. Later, after he discovers her infidelity, he turns petulant. Facing such erratic twists and turns, the reader begins to lose confidence in the novel's consistency. Perhaps one of Aldiss's problems is the first-person narrative, which he uses clumsily in relation to the evolution of the hero's consciousness.

The Malacia Tapestry is also intellectually unsatisfying. One of the book's major concerns—what happens when a society gets overencrusted with tradition—seems inadequately dramatized in the business of Bengtsohn and his zahnoscope. With all due respect to the James Burke theory of cultural evolution, it is hard to believe that such a harmless toy could pose a threat to a highly developed society such as Malacia's.

The narrative may raise a more disturbing question for some readers, namely, what is the purpose of the alternative world setting? As things unfold, the references to the saurian ancestry, the long species history, the odd beasts, and the "flighted people" seem increasingly arbitrary and marginal. Has a promising historical novel about Venice been sacrificed on the altar of science fiction to accommodate such trivial indulgences? Exactly how is the reader expected to position himself or herself in relation to the tone and setting? If our sympathies with Perian de Chirolo wear thin, our curiosity about his world turns to tedium, since its very existence seems artistically unnecessary. Is this view to take too solemn an attitude to what might be a mere entertainment, a jeu d'esprit in which Aldiss plays on the border of traditional genre conventions? Perhaps; yet if Aldiss intended in *The Malacia Tapestry* to unite the serious traditional novel of character and moral transformation with the science fiction subgenre of alternative history, the work is surely flawed for the reasons suggested.

A comparison may be helpful here. *The Malacia Tapestry* resembles in some ways the Russian writer Dimitri Merejkowsky's once well-known *The Romance of Leonardo da Vinci,* published in 1902.[23] In both novels the influence of a powerful artist works on the consciousness of the hero. In both cases we have detailed historical settings and a hero lacking in direction, although Merejkowsky's Giovanni is a timid awestruck puritan, while Aldiss's Perian is a mildly opportunistic epicurean. More to the point, both novels move from realism to fantasy and produce scenes of supernatural visitation that work powerfully on the hero's consciousness. In a historical novel such as Merejkowsky's, however, known history is reimagined and focused through both fictional and historical characters. In the science fiction subgenre of alternative history, real history is imaginatively extended from some key nexus point, as in Philip K. Dick's version of the effects of the supposed victory of the Axis powers in the Second World War in *The Man in the High Castle.* In Aldiss's novel, however, the reader finds reality not once but twice removed. We are confronted with an "an oddness too much"—to use the well-known phrase of C. S. Lewis: an alternative Venice in the foreground, together with a background (and it is really no more than that) in which the human species derives from reptilian ancestors. Whatever the faults of his novel, Merejkowsky's intellectual point is clear and sharp: he seeks to chart an historical change of consciousness, portraying the end of the Christian epoch and the revival of the pagan gods that will usher in the modern world. Aldiss's point is much less clear, and we are distanced in such an idiosyncratic way from the epoch he writes about that the whole enterprise seems less than compelling.

Perhaps, after all, the paperback editions of Malacia betray something of the book's uncertainty and lack of focus. The Panther Books (U.K.) edition contains a few of the Tiepolo illustrations but shows a very strange stylized insectile-reptilian creature on the cover, one that seems to have nothing to do with the contents of Aldiss's narrative. (One can sympathize with the problem of the cover artist: what exactly *is* the book's real focus?) The Ace Books (U.S.) edition also retains a few of the Tiepolo drawings but displays a front-to-back color cover illustration that shows a half-draped beauty (Armida) comforted by one gallant (de Lambant) while another (Perian) attacks a dragon-beast resembling a Tyrannosaurus or Raptor (it's supposed to be a "devil-jaw"). In plain view is a fantasy city on an impossible crag and some elaborately costumed figures on horseback who seem indifferent to the battle. We are told by the Ace blurb that the novel depicts "Renaissance Man in alternative reality," which is perhaps more than Aldiss himself actually conveys to us for a great part of the novel.

Enemies of the System

Aldiss's next mainstream science fiction novel moves us much closer to reality. If *Enemies of the System* (1978) also deals with a static world, it is one very different from the one depicted in the richly embroidered *Malacia Tapestry*.

Enemies of the System was in fact written to answer the Soviet challenge that no western writer would be allowed to portray the Soviet world with completeness and accuracy.[24] The novel is set a million years in the future. Several members of Homo Uniformis—an evolved branch of Homo sapiens—have been sent to the planet Lysenka II for rest and relaxation. With the development of the bio-shunt mechanism, activity occurring within the human autonomic nervous system itself is brought under control of thought systems, "an obvious example is the penile erection, once an involuntary act" (26). The product of this artificial evolution manifests itself in a new political organization of the human species, known as BioCom (Biological Communism). This ideological system insists that the individual at all times suppress self for community. Although such a policy has its benefits, Homo Uniformis has taken this policy to such extremes that the simple matter of voicing any kind of personal opinion is taken as a threat to the stability of the system. To guard against this threat, much communication between people has become a series of slogans and reified expressions such as "our strength lies in our unity" and the title that defines Homo Uniformis, "Man Alike Throughout."

The visitors to Lysenka II, who are on a bus expedition to Dunderzee Gorge, one of the planet's most famous landmarks, encounter some of the primitive inhabitants, creatures who actually evolved from Homo sapiens before the creation of BioCom. Due to limited food resources many of these humans have devolved into various animal states. As the bus advances it comes across a large pit in the road and crashes into it. Confusion and panic ensue as the visitors attempt to come to grips with the situation. The structures of the BioCom system fail to account for such an emergency situation, and several of the group are forced to express individual opinions and to assume leadership roles, much to the shock and discomfort of others. Eventually a small group sets out to find assistance, among them are Sygiek, Kordan, Takeido, Burek, and Dulcifer, all of whom in various ways have so far displayed tendencies to step beyond the restrictions of the system. The female Sygiek possesses an unauthorized gun and uses it to kill several threatening creatures; Dulcifer possesses the initiative to act and is the catalyst for much of the group's actions; and Kordan is a historian who on several occasions seems to speculate upon possible reinterpretations of what is considered official history. However, all of these people tend to jump back in line as soon as they have tested the boundaries of what is permissible within the system. Indeed, another member of the group is the timid travel guide Constanza, who is always there to comment upon the actions of the others. When the Homo sapiens survivors capture the newcomers and lock them within a cage in their cave dwelling, the Homo Uniformis group has the opportunity to observe the behavior of its distant cousins. At one point Takeido expresses admiration for Homo sapiens, for its ability to imagine and fantasize, but the other prisoners denounce such speculations and Constanza in particular accuses him of heresy and covers her ears to avoid hearing these treasonous thoughts. However, Takeido continues: "I just want to say there is another point of view to be put, and in the system it can never be put. . . . If you speak out, you are an enemy of the system. Is our way of life so insecure? Can one question make a whole statement collapse?"[25]

Takeido goes on to say that without imagination Homo Uniformis has failed to progress further in a million years than Homo sapiens did in 100 years. As usual, Aldiss expertly counterpoints versions of reality, effectively contrasting Takeido's passionate speech with the calm reasoning that defines Uniformis. Dulcifer then cautions Takeido, telling him "You will come to understand that it was sapiens' mad unchecked development which was the symptom of something wrong. I daresay that, as you claim, sapiens would have overrun half the galaxy by now. But remember what a mess they made of Earth!" (*Enemies*, 105) The tension in this confrontation is too much for Kordan and he accuses Takeido of sedition and warns that he himself will be in the witness box to convict him.

Finally, the prisoners are led to the site of the cave dwellers' ritual and as part of the ceremony are placed atop a platform. It has become obvious that they are viewed not as prisoners but as gods who have returned from the skies aboard ships like the one that once crashed. However, from the platform, Dulcifer notices an opening in the cave ceiling; he shoots the leader of the primitives with Sygiek's gun and manages to escape to the outside. There he finds members of the Reason Police who have been searching for them and leads them towards the cave. Once the Reason Police arrive, Constanza reveals that she was in fact a secret member of the Police and she has all five tourists arrested. Among the many charges that she accuses them of are hostile logic, deformed thought processes, misapplication of history, pessimism, and collusion with traitors. The novel ends suddenly with the five prisoners being taken away into the night of Lysenka II.

This novel demonstrates that the evolutionary step created by the bio-shunt mechanism precludes any other form of progress. This is social and intellectual entropy indeed, as foreshadowed in Yevgeny Zamyatin's famous novel *We*—which inspired Orwell's *1984*—and is an influence on Aldiss's vision here.[26] The ability to create, to experience, to imagine, is sacrificed by Homo Uniformis in favor of clearly defined and predictable rules of existence.

Enemies of the System was inspired by a visit Aldiss made to Poland in August 1976. As he explains in *The Detached Retina*: "Like many inventions of science fiction, mine was no idle one, but based on a real and horrific Soviet formulation. Soviet medical students used to begin their Latin course with a statement: *'Homo sovieticus sum'* (I am a Soviet man). These future doctors were taught that there were two strains of human being, *Homo sovieticus* and *Homo sapiens*. . . . I was happy to pass on this book to doubters in the West the good news that our political and moral systems, faulty though they may be, are not and never were mirror images of those created in the darker recesses of the Kremlin."[27]

After the dead end of *Malacia* and his uncertain forays into more experimental structures, *Enemies of the System* marked Aldiss's return to the solid mainstream of science fiction. Its level-headedness, its vital connection with important issues, its narrative ease are all impressive. More to the point, however, *Enemies of the System* is an examination of the character and goals of a future society; it raises issues that would surface again, and in a much more comprehensive context, in Aldiss's most ambitious and successful attempt at speculative storytelling, the *Helliconia* series of the early 1980s.

Chapter Three

The *Helliconia* Series: Civilization, Morale, and Structures of Belief

Mankind lies groaning, half-crushed beneath the weight of its own progress. Men do not suffi-
ciently realize that the future is in their hands. Theirs is the task of determining . . .
if they want merely to live, or intend to make just the extra effort required for fulfilling, even on their refractory planet, the essential function of the universe, which is a
machine for the making of gods.

—Henri Bergson, *The Two Sources of Morality and Religion* (1932)

By the close of the 1970s Aldiss had written more than 30 novels and
collections of short stories and had explored in them a wide range of
ideas, without ever resting comfortably in a particular ideology, dogma,
or aesthetic formula. His next major work would be an attempt to
define a larger context within which these (sometimes conflicting) ideas
and visions could be treated in a synthesizing manner. The *Helliconia*
series—he prefers not to think of it as a trilogy—was published during
the early 1980s, and in it we see the culmination of more than three
decades of imaginative thought.[1] The *Helliconia* books perhaps express
most clearly Aldiss's concerns over the state of modern civilization. In
the preface to *Helliconia Spring,* Aldiss explains that he wished to create
in that work "a place much like our world, with only one factor
changed—the length of the year. It was to be a stage of the kind of
drama in which we are embroiled in our century."[2]

The *Helliconia* series grapples with many of the issues, both cultural
and aesthetic, raised in Aldiss's earlier novels and in those of his notable
predecessors, Wells and Stapledon. From the beginning Aldiss had
attempted to establish in his various texts possibilities of order, clusters
of meaning, that might stand against the forces of chance and nature,
against the fright of space and time that so many science fiction writers
evade or trivialize. Like Wells and Stapledon, Aldiss has always been
aware of humankind's lamentable tendency to misuse all of its cultural
tools, from technology to philosophical and spiritual ideas, a fact that

makes social stability impossible and progress throughout history a very doubtful proposition. In the *Helliconia* series, Aldiss attempts to fashion an image of human cultural achievement that includes a sense of wholeness and integration with all life, one that incorporates values that transcend mere stoical acceptance of fate. Such a synthesis, as Aldiss sees it, is necessary to carry Homo sapiens past the negatives implicit in either a traditionally religious or outrightly secular perspective on human development.

As we have seen, in his first major science fiction novel, *Non-Stop*, published in 1958, Aldiss explored the trope of the generational starship so as to demonstrate the degree to which an individual's understanding of self depends upon an understanding of society and environment. As the priest Marapper explains to Complain in that work:

> "We—everything: ponics, Deadways, the forwards people, the whole shoot—are in a sort of container called a Ship, moving from one bit of the world to another. I've told you this time and time again, but you won't grasp it."
>
> "That theory again!" Complain said sullenly. "What if the world is called Ship, or Ship the world, it makes no difference to us."
>
> For some reason the ship theory, well known although generally disregarded in Quarters, upset and frightened him. (*Non-Stop*, 20)

We find this notion of separate, self-enclosed worlds and fearful perspectives both refined and expanded within the larger context of the *Helliconia* series. In this later work, the orbital satellite Avernus is used to link disparate worlds, each peopled with humans who struggle against the challenges of nature and social disintegration. In fact, in *Helliconia*, not only is Aldiss's range of reference extraordinary but issues raised in earlier novels and stories resurface in a new context. Questions of personal identity ("Outside"), environmental decimation ("All the World's Tears"), the role of science in society (*Frankenstein Unbound*), nuclear war (*Moreau's Other Island*), deterministic fatalism (*The Eighty Minute Hour*), cultural stagnation (*The Malacia Tapestry*), and the breakdown of technology ("Who can replace a Man?") represent only a partial list of Aldiss's themes. In the *Helliconia* series Aldiss moves to the broadest possible context to ask the difficult question: what makes a successful civilization?

Finding some path toward a deeper understanding of human life in society leads Aldiss back to the most fundamental questions about the human place in nature. As he himself explains in a note to his son in

Helliconia Winter, "Why do individuals of the human race long for close community with each other, and yet remain so often apart? Could it be that the isolating factor is similar to that which makes us feel, as a species, apart from the rest of nature?" (392).

The *Helliconia* series is the story of a series of civilizations, each of which struggles to survive the effects of the planet's seasonal extremes. Aldiss uses his imaginary planet to create an ingenious model displaying both the possibilities of growth and change and the danger of cultural stagnation. Since every winter on Helliconia is in reality an ice age, communities are instinctively forced into a protective cocoon. Where the dynamism of human creativity and ingenuity weakens, Helliconia's civilizations face the danger of submitting to the temptations of comfortable repetition, sinking into an existence determined by ancestral ritual and dogma. The reification of customary beliefs over creative thought and expression necessarily leads to a world of structural rigidity in which an outdated cultural ideology becomes dangerously persuasive.

Helliconia's difficulties are caused by its location within a binary star system. The planet orbits a small sunlike star named Batalix, and together they follow an elliptical orbit around the star Freyr that takes 3000 years to complete, a process referred to by the Helliconians as a "Great Year" (Aldiss's pointed evocation of ancient mythology). Freyr is 15 times larger than the sun and 60,000 times as luminous and is responsible for producing the wide range of temperatures experienced on Helliconia. This planet is the home of two seemingly opposed sentient races. The phagors are Helliconia's winter race, product of an age when only Batalix was present in the sky. Humans developed later when the entire solar system was trapped by the gravitational pull of Freyr. Better suited to warmer conditions, humans soon evolved to the point where they were able to compete with the phagors for control of Helliconia.

Helliconia Spring begins with an account of humanity's struggle to survive in the depths of winter when the balance of power is shifted in the phagors' favor. When winter's harshness is moderated by the approach of spring, however, the small human settlement of Oldorando begins to flourish. As environmental conditions change, the community finds itself in a constant struggle to adapt. Although Oldorando is successful at first, a growing population and new scientific discoveries eventually erode the traditional structures that have long kept the community together. Certain individuals leave Oldorando to find answers to personal questions, whereupon a large phagorian army attacks the weakened town and destroys it.

Helliconia Summer shifts its focus to the nations of Borlien and Pannoval. Warm summer temperatures have encouraged larger human empires, safe from phagor attack. However, without the constant phagor threat to define their purpose or an internal or external framework to replace it, the population has lost much of its focus in life and has become disaffected and listless. Under these conditions the human capacity for compassion and understanding is extremely low, and treachery, war, and deceit are the result. Again, because of this weakened condition of human civilization, the phagors are able to destroy much of what the humans have built. The third volume, *Helliconia Winter,* explores the continent of Sibornal and its preparations for the approaching winter. Sibornal is the home of Helliconia's most progressive human civilization and both the scientific discoveries it has made and its favorable geographic location have allowed it to survive the extremes of the Great Year relatively unharmed. Thus Sibornal emerges every spring as the dominant military and cultural power. However, faced with a deteriorating climate, societal unrest, and a sense of fatalism inspired by the waxing and waning of Freyr's presence, the Sibornalese government has lost faith in its religious and political structures and finally gives in to fear and doubt. It invokes a series of repressive edicts aimed at arbitrarily restricting ethnic populations and at eliminating those that are deemed by the government as responsible for the worsening conditions. These restrictions are imposed despite the fact that the government fully understands the scientific reasons for the approaching winter.

Each of these three civilizations is faced with a struggle to locate itself in relation to outside forces, both natural and cultural. In each case it is the failure to deal with the implications of such relationships that signals a particular society's demise. Although most of the story occurs on an alien planet, the *Helliconia* series is really about Earth's own need for a heightened sense of self-awareness. Aldiss structures his book to make this clear. Set beside the *Helliconia* story there is also another narrative (presented in italics) that describes the story of Earth and its far distant observation satellite named Avernus. Earth has suffered from a full-scale spiritual crisis. Its faith in technology has produced a massive nuclear war that has eliminated nearly all human life. Meanwhile, the spaceship Avernus, another manifestation of Earth's technocentric culture, has been dispatched to observe Helliconia, the only planet besides Earth found to support complex life forms. It is through the relationship that develops between Earth, the Avernus, and Helliconia that Aldiss explores his solution to the problem of human interconnectedness.

Ingeniously, Aldiss uses the Avernus to demonstrate how narrative itself can be a source of spiritual awareness in offering the possibility of dialogue between text and the reader. Reading is necessarily a creative act, one that depends both upon our own receptivity and on the potential input of some external source. Listening to the stories of others, we become connected with them and achieve some understanding of ourselves. This example of a basic human need to experience life as "meaningful connectedness," Aldiss implies, is the very essence of spiritual existence. Watching the unfolding drama of Helliconia's civilizations from their auditoria, Earth's inhabitants participate in an interstellar discourse. The stream of data sent by the Avernians is transformed into a social text, and as the generations pass, Earth's humans create out of this continuing narrative the truths that help them understand their world. This process is paralleled by the reader who explores the narrative that Aldiss himself has provided. The Avernians, however, are left out of this fundamentally regenerative relationship. Not able to return to Earth (due to the immensity of space) nor to land on Helliconia (due to the presence of a lethal virus to which they have no immunity), they are completely isolated and soon begin to degenerate into barbarism. By introducing these parallels between Earth and Helliconia, Aldiss is able to raise the epistemological and ontological issues that frame any analysis of what constitutes a spiritual existence. What kind of knowledge is relevant? What is my relation to other living things, to my community, to my environment? How am I connected to the natural world that surrounds me? These questions are the oldest and most fundamental ones that human beings have asked, and the answers remain as elusive and nebulous as ever. Unfortunately, while science and technology can be a constructive force, they have often been used in a manner that actually prevents us from discovering satisfying answers to these questions.

In his deployment of Helliconia's various civilizations Aldiss repeatedly demonstrates that, for a developing people, the most important and natural relationship is that which exists between the individual and the cosmic principle of order, or deity.[3] This relationship forms the essential tissue of connectedness required in order for the individual to coexist with others and with the environment. When this relational structure loses its dynamism or becomes rigid and repressive, other means must be found to ensure the social morale that promotes order and altruism. Throughout the series Aldiss probes the connection between belief, stability, and group harmony. Ultimately he suggests that what enables humans to overcome their grasping individualism and to meet the challenges put to them by nature is a belief in something that transcends humanity and that offers a core of meaning, resulting in a dialogue in time between successive individuals and groups and the *mysterium* itself. Furthermore, the acceptance of a unifying superior principle works to make possible the reconciliation of divergent groups and nations within a common human community. Aldiss suggests that when religious frameworks collapse or are prematurely obliterated, the secular order may not be sufficient to prevent communities from dissolving in violence and chaos.

As Helliconia's seasons slowly complete their century-long cycle, the reader witnesses a corresponding shift in the dominant religious form. In fact, each of the *Helliconia* novels focuses almost entirely on a particular form of worship and defines the specific civilization that helps sustain that worship.

Despite brief episodes foregrounding the advent of gods who will come to dominate Helliconia in the future, *Helliconia Spring* is concerned primarily with the figure of Wutra and the ritual that attaches to him. As the Great Year unfolds, *Helliconia Summer* shifts focus to Akha, the great one, while *Helliconia Winter* defines the conditions leading to the worship of God the Azoiaxic. These three major religions represent the dominant spiritual practices that Helliconia's human populations have developed. The character of each belief system in a certain sense defines the limits of the civilization that produces it, yet all three are responses to the unique challenges posed by the natural order in which they arise.

While Helliconia's religions are located along a continuum of development, the belief systems of Earth's humans and of those aboard the Avernus run along directly opposing paths. For the Avernus crew all things must be understood empirically. The Avernus is the greatest achievement of a society that placed its faith in the power of scientific method and technology. Critical of this point of view, which has nearly destroyed them, the survivors of Earth's nuclear war carry out a spiritual revolution that asserts the universality and oneness of organisms within a particular biosphere. These postcatastrophe humans develop this philosophy by learning from the mistakes made by their ancestors and out of the empathy they develop for the inhabitants of distant Helliconia. This transplanetary empathy draws its inspiration from the cosmic interconnectedness suggested by the figure of Gaia. Aldiss bases this figure upon the ideas of the scientist James Lovelock, first put forth in 1969 and systematically stated in his 1979 book, *Gaia: A New Look at Life on Earth.*[4]

According to Lovelock's first ideas, Gaia is a planet-sized organism that spontaneously responds and adapts to the changing aspects of its environment. For example, should Gaia receive an increased amount of sunlight, it would develop vegetation that would reflect away the excess heat in order to keep the temperature constant. In this context, humanity might be understood as a phenomenon created by Gaia in order to help maintain its overall planetary balance. Should humans endanger that balance Gaia would presumably develop some means of reducing the effects of human influence. Aldiss makes considerable use of this theory in order to explain the evolution of consciousness, which might be seen an instrument of planetary fine-tuning and self-reflection, as proposed in the speculations of Olaf Stapledon and in *The Phenomenon of Man* by the Jesuit philosopher Teilhard de Chardin. The human need for contact with others is the active principle that expresses this fundamental striving toward oneness of consciousness. This oneness may be seen as a secular equivalent to the old religious notion of a connection between the individual human soul and the divine, through recognition of the principle of Atman, the spirit within, which links the individual with Brahman, the ground of being. Clearly, in such a context, individual human happiness and success is dependent upon the establishment of a sense of harmony within, but the within is connected with something greater—the community, the planet, the cosmos itself.

Such concepts are by no means the only ones that Aldiss draws upon to create his world, however. Given the link he establishes between seasonal imagery and the rise and fall of civilizations, one might at first sight imagine that in the *Helliconia* series Aldiss had produced yet another Spenglerian scenario for science fiction. (James Blish, for example, in *Cities in Flight,* drew upon the work of Oswald Spengler).[5] An even more potent influence on Aldiss, however, is Arnold Toynbee, whose famous and much-discussed book, *A Study of History* (1934–1961), was a major force in British intellectual life for at least the first decade of Aldiss's writing career.[6] Toynbee's position, which was to reject the determinism of Spengler while insisting on the importance of both tradition and of creative change, is clearly compatible with the Aldiss perspective, in which the inner life, personal responsibility, the recovery of links with tradition, and the power to adapt creatively to new conditions are potent elements.

In Toynbee's view, if a civilization is to progress, it must make appropriate responses to particular challenges.[7] Meeting these challenges, which are by no means merely physical, helps a society achieve a level of self-determination, fostering an inner spiritual strength that enables further successful responses to be made. Should the creative minorities within a given society fail to respond to such challenges, that civilization will stagnate, force will rule, and collapse at last becomes inevitable. Unlike many rationalist historians, Toynbee recognized religion as a key factor in the development and sustenance of every civilization. Religion, he insisted, was an integral part of human social development, and he used it to help explain the rise and fall of various civilizations, such as the Hellenic civilization of Greece and Rome.[8] Toynbee attributed the fall of the classical Greek civilization to its inability to respond to the challenges that would move it beyond its belief in the primacy of the city-state, an adept human creation but one that lacked reference to a universal principle. He argued that, without such development, classical Greece could not successfully cope with the challenges of its increasing populations and intercity conflict. In other words, without the development of a synthesizing higher religion, the necessary structures for societal progress were unavailable to the Greeks (Toynbee, 4). Toynbee also suggests that part of the origin of certain crises in modern Western societies, such as Nazism and World War Two, can be directly associated with the rejection of religious values and the substitution of a secular for a spiritual focus.

Toynbee argues that there are three varieties of human worship: the worship of nature, the worship of man, and the worship of an absolute reality or God (Toynbee, 1). Primitive humankind expresses its spirituality in connection with phenomena observed in nature such as the sun, moon, and various animals. However, as societies acquire control over the forces of nature and begin to understand the mysteries of its operation, the worship of man becomes more prevalent. This worship of man is expressed through obedience to godlike, mostly male, rulers and through the belief in the divinity of human institutions. As a society begins to aspire to an existence beyond the physical necessities, it must reject these egocentric and human-centered visions. Humanity now has the opportunity to reach toward that which is greater than itself and to attempt to develop a relationship with some form of transcendent reality. This sense of a universal spiritual power carries the potential, Toynbee asserts, for a belief in social interconnectedness and human unity, beliefs that are necessary for advanced civilizations to survive (Toynbee, 4). Toynbee designates Christianity, Islam, Hinduism, and Buddhism as higher religions, on the grounds that each of them affirms the existence of a transcendent God, one who supplies a moral framework of compassion and brotherhood with which to structure a particular society.[9] It is the reach and potency of these belief systems, Toynbee argues, that underlies the foundation of the great universal civilizations.

Aldiss's treatment of the relationship between belief and civilization throughout the *Helliconia* novels corresponds very closely to Toynbee's analysis of the various stages of spiritual development. If we apply a Toynbean framework, the apparent chaos of religious activity on Helliconia assumes a decidedly cohesive form. The religions of Aldiss's fictional world pass through three stages, moving from nature-worship toward the affirmation of an exalted humanity; in the end they reach the notion of God as a transcendent and universal power. Although these broad categories certainly apply, it is important to note that there is much interaction between Helliconia's three primary civilizations and that they share many common characteristics. Since it is typical of Aldiss to entertain seemingly contradictory ideas within a text and to attempt to create fictional characters that are more than mere stereotypes, one would expect him to have a lively sense of the complexity required to create credible imaginary civilizations, and in fact, none of the societies in Helliconia exists as a static or enclosed entity—Aldiss is very careful to document various developments and changes within them. However, it can still be demonstrated that each culture adheres to a dominant ideological construct, one that is connected with a particular relationship to its divinity. The development of this relationship structures scientific, social, and philosophical advances, so that the absence of a relevant spiritual framework means decline and social disintegration.

Despite all these links between Toynbee's vision of history and the themes and structures of Aldiss's *Helliconia* books, we must note one major divergence. Whereas Toynbee suggests that a renewal and transformation of Christianity could be the solution to the ills of humankind (or at least the answer to the malaise of western society), Aldiss, following in the steps of Stapledon in particular, believes that yet another level of spiritual achievement is possible.[10] In *Helliconia Winter* Aldiss suggests that the worship of an externalized, all-powerful God is not enough, that without an accompanying empirical perspective, this approach can actually invite doubt and resistance, leading to a deepened spiritual crisis. While both Aldiss and Toynbee are dismayed by the dogma that so frequently accompanies religious belief, Aldiss is less certain than Toynbee of the ability of traditional religions to rid themselves of this component, which, like Toynbee, he deems stultifying. As Marvin Perry argues in his critical analysis of Toynbee, a religion that relies upon external gods "offers no rational explanations; it does not clarify the mystery of man but relates a story of sin and salvation that transcends objective knowledge."[11] Indeed, many would argue that a return to traditional theological principles is unworkable in a postindustrial world, yet the need for spiritual awareness, for a connection between self and other, seems all the more pressing. In explaining his approach to this very problem, Aldiss writes, "I did not think God or a god was a strong enough or a "modern" enough link between two seemingly opposed sides of the equation. . . . This time, I had an answer. The "god" was the planet, was nature, was process."[12] Here we see how Aldiss combines the Toynbean perspective with the ideas he derives from Lovelock's early pronouncements. In Aldiss's vision of the planet as deity, transcendence is achieved through the development of worship to the point where it reaches out to embrace the universal mother, Gaia, a symbol of human dependency on nature. The *Helliconia* novels are an attempt to describe the processes necessary to reach this state of higher planetary consciousness, a synthesis that is urgently required by the new race of humans on earth, the survivors of the great atomic war.

Wutra

In the prelude to *Helliconia Spring*, the reader is introduced to the figures of Yuli and Wutra. Yuli, son of Alehaw, is portrayed as a mythic hero, a cultural hero in fact, one who will lead the infant civilization out of darkness, a man to be revered by future generations as the father of Oldorando's society. He is what Toynbee refers to as a conquering creative spirit, able to meet the challenges of a changing environment in a manner that forges the framework for an emerging consciousness. Yuli's youth is spent as a hunter-gatherer in the Barrier mountains, and there he learns to worship Wutra, god of the skies. Of the three major religions practiced by the Helliconians, the worship of Wutra is the least detailed and most nebulous. This is appropriate, since it is the most primitive of Helliconia's three major religions. Based upon the worship of nature, it possesses (and requires) a very minimal structure and organization. (Aldiss clearly draws upon ideas and images from the Indo-European beginnings of western religion, combining these ideas with some aspects of early Sumerian and Hebraic culture).[13]

Wutra in fact is the "bringer of light" (*Spring*, 45), and has under his control the twin sentinels Batalix and Freyr. As a nature religion, Wutra-worship is used by Helliconia's primitive societies to explain the wide range of temperatures they experience throughout the great year. While the other two Helliconian religions assist people in dealing with the difficulties brought about by the wide range of temperatures, the Wutra religion only attempts to explain the *causes* of this natural phenomenon. Wutra provides little motivation for his followers to make concrete responses to the challenge of extreme weather, a motivation that only appears in the religions that dominate the nations of Pannoval and Sibornal.

The Wutra mythology is elemental. Wutra's faithful envision him as taking part in a great war, and the cold of Helliconia's winter is caused by Wutra's absence while he is occupied with these greater matters. Even the winter clouds are explained within the context of Wutra's efforts; "their lives were solitary, hidden frequently behind cloud which was the billowing smoke from Wutra's war" (*Spring*, 20). At one point, Yuli recalls an ancient chant that was used by his people to help explain the fading of Freyr's strength and the advance of the clouds:

Wutra in sorrow
Will put Freyr to barrow
And us to the billow (*Spring*, 21)

Although Wutra is personalized, he is intrinsically associated with the natural processes of the sky. Unlike Akha, with whom he is said to battle, Wutra is never imagined to exist beyond the confines of the natural world. He is a figure of causation, explaining only that which is seen and not understood. He possesses no transcendent powers, nor does his worship help humanity to understand the processes that lie beyond the most fundamental physical observations. The hope he brings is one based upon superstition, and the imagery that surrounds him reflects the struggles and hardships of his followers. Thus, Wutra wanders the skies in constant search for his enemies, reflecting the nomadic nature of the hunter-gatherer society to which he belongs.

Because of its relatively primitive structure, worship of Wutra is rather stunted in the moral dimension. Wutra's inability to provide a sufficient framework for complex issues of good and evil eventually renders him obsolete and ineffective as a source of spiritual health. Toynbee believes that all men possess "a vein of diabolical evil" that is responsible for self-centeredness and for the tendency towards warfare and violence that human societies display.[14] Explaining this struggle between good and evil within human consciousness is a fundamental function of religious worship and one that Wutra satisfies only in the most primitive hunter societies. Indeed, Yuli eventually rationalizes that Wutra's absence from the world is not only the product of his great battle but also signifies his displeasure with his followers. Yuli remembers one of the legends he had listened to round his father's fire. The elders had spoken of how men on earth had once offended the God of the Skies, who refused to bestow his warmth on the earth. Now the sentinels watched for the hour when Wutra might return; they hoped for a time when he might regard earth with more affection. This affection, however, would be dependent upon human behavior. If the god found that humanity had improved its conduct, he then would remove the frosts (*Spring,* 58). Such a binary framework of right and wrong, warmth and cold, can no longer help Yuli once he departs from the family circle and enters into a wider social sphere. Yuli is forced to suppress this primitive moral aspect of Wutra worship after he murders two traders from Pannoval. Although his actions arose out of necessity, Yuli's conscience cannot rest after this crime. Unconsciously he fears that the evil within him may be partly responsible for Wutra's banishment. As a means of compensation he rejects his parents' faith and labels his ancestral religion as savagery. To compensate for this loss of direction Yuli turns to the earth god Akha, for he is "astonished at the confusion within himself" (*Spring,* 57).

The old structures of Yuli's native faith are unable to provide what a more complex civilization requires; compassion, forgiveness, and security of belonging. After making his decision to enter the priesthood of Akha, "Yuli thought in terms of great joy that he had found an amazing faith" and that the "confusions within would be banished by greater knowledge" (*Spring,* 58). His entrance into the priesthood initially serves the role he seeks. The clergy, being fully aware of Yuli's crime, insist that he admit to his guilt before becoming a priest; he does so and achieves a new level of self-awareness. His confessions to Father Sifans reveal to him a new approach towards the nature of sin. Sin no longer forces one away from the object of worship, thus destroying that most fundamental relationship, but actually, since it is inevitable, can be used to bring one closer to god. As Father Sifans states: "That unhappy incident of the murders is now sealed behind the wall of the past. Yet you must never allow yourself to forget it, lest, in forgetting, you come to believe that it never happened. Like the many suburbs of Pannoval, all things in life are interwoven. Your sin and your longing to serve Akha are of a piece. Did you imagine that it was holiness that led a man to serve Akha? Not so. Sin is a more powerful mover" (*Spring,* 68). Yuli's newfound faith proves abortive, since it is in conflict with too many of the beliefs he adhered to before encountering the rigid structures of Pannoval. Nevertheless, Yuli's experience in Pannoval reaffirms his faith in human relationships, recently destroyed by what he perceived as his father's betrayal. With a returned sense of hope and purpose, he successfully travels through the Quzint mountains to found a new civilization. Although this new community retains the fundamental beliefs of Wutra worship, it rids itself of such formal systems as the priesthood, leaving it more flexible and capable of progress under the rapidly changing conditions of spring. Soon however, advancing science and technology come into conflict with the basic principles that make belief in Wutra possible. As we shall see, without the development of alternative spiritual frameworks, the failure of Wutra must necessarily coincide with the failure of the society that worships him.

With the passing of several generations and the advent of spring, belief in Wutra becomes an increasingly cumbersome appendage, forcing a view of existence that is no longer spiritually or intellectually fulfilling. According to Toynbee, the only means for a society to prosper is for it to make an appropriate response to a particular challenge, and Oldorando possesses a creative minority that attempts to do just that. In the section entitled "Embruddock," Shay Tal raises questions that have been ignored by her ancestors throughout the great winter:

> Some disaster happened in the past. The long past. So complete was it that no one now can tell you what it was or how it came about. We know only that it brought darkness and cold of long duration. . . . It may have happened long ago yet it infects every day of our lives. It ages us, it wears us out, it devours us, it tears our children from us. It makes us not only ignorant but in love with ignorance. . . . We have to piece together what has happened to reduce us to this chilly farmyard; then we can improve our lot, and see to it that the disaster does not befall us and our children again. (*Spring,* 129)

Toynbee argues that throughout the greater part of history primitive societies survived only on the basis of what previous generations had taught them—the status quo prevailed. Civilizations as such developed when creative personalities turned away from custom and led the uncreative majority towards self-determination and societal growth. Both Yuli and Shay Tal exemplify this power and they are directly responsible for many of the achievements of Oldorando society. Yet the strength of Shay Tal's creative spirit is the result of her faith in community and the importance she places on the development of healthy relationships. To this end she establishes the Academy and spurns the advances of Aoz Roon, knowing that he would restrict her role within the community. Shay Tal's experiments with agriculture are a direct example of how technology can be used to meet particular challenges successfully. Her research is used to raise the standard of living for an entire community and has the potential to rejuvenate Oldorando's ailing sense of spirituality. Unfortunately, as Marvin Perry explains, for "the great mass of people . . . civilization is only a thin veneer," and when the direction afforded by their leaders is removed, society faces the constant danger of disintegration.[15] Thus, Shay Tal's decision to move to Sibornal symbolizes the failure of the cultural balance she attempted to establish and foretells the imminent collapse of Oldorando's civilization. Her departure is in part caused by those elements in society—generally powerful male figures—who have little to gain from an increase in societal standards and from the instability that seems to be associated with change itself. Aoz Roon, Tanth Ein, and Raynil Layan represent the old guard, exerting their influence through the will-to-power and domination rather than through creativity and cooperation.

Raynil Layan, for example, accepts the emerging scientific advancements of his society but uses them to further his own well-being rather than that of the community. He symbolizes the fragmentation brought upon a people who have lost touch with unifying creative symbols. This attitude is manifested in his failure to defend Oldorando during the phagor attack; "understand that I left, not of course for my own sake, but for the sake of those I had a duty to protect" (*Spring,* 552). Toynbee notes that the turning from a period of social growth to one of social disintegration is not the result of a lack of creative spark but takes place when a "creator is called upon to play the part of the savior who comes to the rescue of a society that has failed to respond because the challenge has worsted a minority that has ceased to be creative and that has sunk into being merely dominant" (Toynbee, 6:177). Should this savior figure accept the role of "rear guard," a civilization may receive a reprieve from imminent collapse. Instead, Raynil Layan uses his leadership role and knowledge to coerce Dathka into seizing military control of the city, resulting in panic and rioting. As his appearance suggests, Raynil Layan proves to be a serpentine antihero with "his forked beard . . . tied with two ribbons, in a manner he had learned from foreigners" (*Spring,* 462). Appropriately, he betrays the origins of the Wutra religion in the phagor worship to Dathka; this betrayal in itself demonstrates the severity of Oldorando's spiritual crisis and underscores the fact that without belief in a transcendent reality, morality and order soon disintegrate. Dathka's reaction to Raynil Layan's revelation reveals the backlash and resulting crisis effected by a lack of religious grounding:

> "Wutra a Phagor? It can't be. You go too far. This damned learning—it can make white black. All such nonsense stems from the academy. I'd kill it. If I had the power I'd kill it."
> "If you want power, I'll side with you," said Raynil Layan. (*Spring,* 525)

What is amiss here is not that a sensitive religious issue has been raised, but that the effect of this discussion is not to further develop or challenge belief but merely to raise the question of how this issue affects state politics. Religion is no longer an experience, a dynamic force, but simply one of the elements to be manipulated by those in search of power. Opportunism and pragmatism, however, are no substitute for a powerful mythos capable of structuring all aspects of life and complex enough to provide a moral basis for individual action.[16] As we shall see, this scene is in essence repeated with the fall of the civilizations in *Helliconia Summer* and *Helliconia Winter*. It represents the ultimate irony that the stability religion produces leads to the very learning that ultimately seems to unseat the original belief system.[17] The question becomes whether or not this conundrum is inescapable. Is there, in other words, some ultimate spiritual truth, or system of belief, that allows one to progress intellectually without simultaneously disproving one's underlying belief system? While Toynbee appears satisfied that this question is answered positively by the traditional notions of faith that underlie Christianity, Aldiss concludes that what is required is an as-yet-undiscovered religion that satisfies both our intellectual and spiritual needs. One of the central achievements of the *Helliconia* series is to explore the relationship between spiritual crisis and societal breakdown, to probe the connections between human happiness and human belief in transcendent power. The thoroughgoing manner in which Aldiss addresses this question, and his depth of focus on it, gives these volumes a formidable intellectual reach and relates them to one of the central existential questions of our age.

Akhanaba

Helliconia Summer, the second volume of the *Helliconia* series, focuses upon the societies that worship Akhanaba, the great one. This religion broadly embraces those characteristics of belief that Toynbee defines as the worship of man, and this worship has a direct impact upon both the development and decline of these communities. The glimpse of Akha worship we receive in *Helliconia Spring* foreshadows the dominance this religion acquires throughout most civilized regions of Campannlat during the summer phase. It is clear that in the equatorial climate of Campannlat, belief in Akha fulfills certain conditions that are favorable to social progress. Primary among these conditions is that Akha worship is structured so as to impart an ideology of self-preservation, one that seeks to encourage human self-shielding against the damaging extremes of the environment. While the Sibornalese deity, God the Azoiaxic, also performs this role, there is a fundamental difference between the way these roles are carried out. Akha protects his subjects through things physical, through the land itself, whereas the Azoiaxic, product of a more advanced religion, protects through social, spiritual, and emotional means as well. Although the Akhanaban faith also attempts to address these internal psychological issues, the rapidly changing society that it governs soon renders it ineffectual in dealing with these concerns, much as Wutra failed to serve Yuli many generations before.

Akhanaba is the god of earth and the underground and his worshippers are afforded protection from the extremes of temperature that characterize life on the planet surface. The sky is seen as the enemy, bringing freezing winds in winter and intolerable heat during summer. With the protection derived from their underground dwellings, Akha's followers are capable of creating a sustainable culture, one that can survive the rigors of winter without losing the knowledge acquired from previous generations. To preserve this knowledge, Pannoval, the center of Akha worship, is constructed so as to divide society into various levels and to assign defined roles to its members, a system that is at once functional and repressive. The cave complex below the Quzint mountains provides an environment that allows for a caste system to succeed, through isolation, secrecy, and protection from external influences. To maintain this existence Pannoval's citizens learn a variety of religious verses:

> Skies give false prospects,
> Skies shower extremes,
> Against all such schemes
> Akha's earth overhead protects.
>
> (*Spring,* 58)

Heretics who voice their opposition to these beliefs are silenced quickly in order to sustain a system that grows fragile as the extremes in temperature worsen in summer and winter. Pannoval's priesthood recognizes the necessity of a spiritual focus in order for its citizens' efforts to be directed towards the survival of the community. As Perry notes, in Toynbee's schema, it is not the environment in and of itself that is responsible for a society's achievements, but the way in which its citizens transform and use it for their own benefit.[18]

Despite these advances, the worship of Akha is inherently limited in its ability to produce a fully developed civilization. Underlying these deficiencies is its human-centered view of religion—the second of Toynbee's three levels of religious development. This view limits the ability of Akhanaba's followers to meet further challenges, since it is essentially inward-looking and narcissistic. The cultures that worship Akha view their leaders as gods, and these leaders, like the god-kings of ancient Egypt, wield an inordinate amount of power. As we shall see, although the Sibornalese encounter a similar problem, it is not an integral part of their religion, but a perversion of it. However, the factional nature of Akha worship inevitably establishes a hierarchy that designates its leaders as a separate segment of humanity.

In *Helliconia Summer,* the most visible of these leaders is JandolAnganol, king of Borlien, and much of the novel focuses upon his well-intentioned yet ineffectual attempts to lead his people forward through Borlien's political union with the neighboring nations of Oldorando and Pannoval. Although JandolAnganol believes this union will create stability and prosperity for his people, his pride prevents him from taking advantage of certain possibilities offered to him by CaraBansity, SartoriIrvrash, and others. Despite his many protestations to Akha, the king recognizes only political and military (that is, human-oriented) solutions to what are in fact spiritual and intellectual problems.

Toynbee refers to this stage of political and military activity as the creation of a universal state, an act that generally occurs after a civilization has already begun to break down. This stage is a stalling tactic, enabling a society to "enjoy a brief 'Indian summer' before its final dissolution" (Toynbee, 1:243). Despite the possibility of imminent collapse, Toynbee acknowledges that the one positive aspect of universal states is their ability to produce the "universal church," an institution that can potentially outlast the state and eventually provide a future society with a still higher religion (Toynbee, 6:171).

JandolAnganol clearly understands the importance of religion to his political aspirations, yet he does not perceive the dangers of his own authoritarian approach. He wishes to reify the present system rather than to allow his faith, and the system of government it inspires, to evolve into something more appropriate to present conditions:

> Throughout his life, since his adolescent years in a Pannovalan monastery, religion had ruled him. Equally, he ruled through religion. Religion held most of his court and his people in thrall. It was the common worship of Akhanaba which united Borlien, Oldorando, and Pannoval into an uneasy alliance. Without Akhanaba there would be only chaos, and the enemies of civilization would prevail. (*Summer,* 38)

This merger of religion with human institutions is central to what Toynbee refers to as the "worship of man," yet the rise of such superficial alliances leads to standardization, which is, as Toynbee explains, generally an unsuccessful response to crisis. If differentiation is the natural outcome of a series of successful responses to a series of different challenges, standardization is no less manifestly the natural outcome of a series of unsuccessful responses to a single challenge, which monotonously continues to present itself so long as it remains unanswered (Toynbee, 6:322).

This unanswered challenge is the inability of the Akhanaban faith to explain and cope with the increasing intensity of Freyr's light and the damage this light causes to Helliconia's populations. While making a public appearance, JandolAnganol, king of Borlien, is greeted with the disturbing cries of approaching apocalypse; "THE FIRE IS COMING: THE OCEANS WILL BURN . . . LIVE WITH AKHA OR DIE FOREVER WITH FREYR" (*Summer,* 34).

Here we approach an apocalyptic moment that threatens the end of time itself. In modern western society, apocalyptic thought inevitably views the present as a time of crisis and congruently as a time of great and imminent expectation.[19] Aldiss's use of apocalyptic language and symbols here gives voice to this feeling of crisis and expectation, mediating the tension that exists between the two. In the terms of Frederick Kreuzinger, this type of prophecy judges and consoles; it also guides a community through the dark times, telling in symbol and story of the end of the old and of the coming of the new.[20] The people of Borlien therefore recognize the approaching collapse of their society yet anticipate that their leaders will make a successful response to the approaching crisis. Their current god, Akhanaba, provides only the most primitive form of physical protection and lacks the ability to give hope and meaning to the changing environment. Akha's focus on things physical produces a ritualization of self-inflicted physical torture believed by his followers to be a means of purging one's sins. The failing relationship between Akha and his followers has destroyed his ability to instill a sense of well-being through discursive means. Thus, JandolAnganol rejects spiritual activities such as prayer (or pauk), and exalts dubious rituals, demonstrating his failure to understand connection. In *Helliconia Winter*, Aldiss makes it clear that the means to an improved society is through empathy, a sense of compassion and understanding for others. For adherents to the Akhanaban faith, solutions to inner conflict are not found by looking beyond one's own existence, but by turning one's gaze inwardly in a spiritually, and physically, self-destructive fashion.

JandolAnganol is the ultimate personification of this malfunction within the Akhanaban framework. He embodies the paradox of a man who through his fanatical devotion to the god alienates himself to such an extent that he himself ultimately fails to integrate within society. In the hope of strengthening his nation he divorces his queen, drives away his son, banishes his chief advisor SartoriIrvrash, imprisons his father, and murders those opposed to him in court. He is a man who constantly bemoans that he is not understood yet shows little ability himself to entertain dialogue with others. Indeed, CaraBansity tells the king of these truths only to have them rejected:

> Your place is in your own kingdom, never more so than now . . . your rightful Queen is here. Fall before her and ask forgiveness. Tear up Esomberr's bill before her eyes. Take back what you love most. Your sanity lies in her. Reject the cozzening of Pannoval . . . win back your son. Kick out Pannoval, kick out the phagor guard, live a saner life with your queen. Reject the false Akhanaba, who has led you. (*Summer,* 443)

These final words are received with violent rage and CaraBansity is thereafter banished from the king's presence. Her words are in reality a plea to the king to empathize with those he loves and lead through that example, rather than through the obscure political unions he attempts to devise in the name of stability. CaraBansity recognizes what the king does not; that progressive change, not stability, is needed, that he requires intimate and personal associations, not structural and political ones. The Akhanaban faith has failed the king. It has failed to provide him with an ability to perceive and respond to the needs and wants of others, of those who look upon him as their savior figure. He under-

stands his environment from his own self-centered location and therefore embraces only his own monologic truths. The violence of his reaction to his advisor's suggestion is characteristic of his intolerance for
those who fail to share in his vision and expresses the magnitude of the
inner conflict that he represses. JandolAnganol has never moved beyond
a childlike, egoistic stage, and thus, CaraBansity observes, "Sire, I
believe the acting principle of your life to be lust rather than love" (*Summer,* 442). This lust is the ultimate expression of the king's inability to
postpone personal gratification, the failure to give consideration to the
needs of others.

The king's deficiencies are not compensated for by the religion that
has ruled him since youth and structured his approach to power. In an
intriguing juxtaposition, Aldiss uses various Christian tropes to ground
the Akhanaban faith in reality and thus distances himself from Toynbee's assertion that Christianity could serve as a successful spiritual
framework for an advanced society. This distance enables Aldiss to focus
upon how Christian institutions, having lost their relevance to modern
issues, have become self-serving and dysfunctional. This examination
allows him to further the theme of man as focus of worship, expressed
by JandolAnganol himself; "Great Akhanaba in the glory of his contra-
dictions: the Two-in-one, man and god, child and beast, temporal and
eternal, spirit and stone" (*Summer,* 37). As we have seen, this description
applies to the king as well as it does to Akhanaba. The entire structure
of the Pannovalan church takes on Christian overtones, and its sectarian
structure reminds one of the highly stratified organization of the Roman
Catholic Church. Aldiss even makes the issue of divorce a central concern of the novel, echoing actual history: we recall that it was a marital
crisis that helped Henry the Eighth ensure the objectives of his realpoli-
tik and paved the way for the unholy fusion of politics and religion in
Cromwell's England. In *Helliconia Summer,* the king says, "My unbend-
ing intention is to divorce myself from Queen MyrdemInggala by a bill
of divorcement issued by the Great C'Sarr Kilander IX, Head of the
Holy Pannovalan Empire and Father Supreme of the Church of Akhanaba, whose servants we are." (34)

At this phase of history religion no longer aspires to answer life's
great questions but has become merely a political structure, a means of
keeping the citizenry in line. The people of Borlien are never seen to
contemplate and enter into communion with their god, and consequently they consistently fail in their human relationships as well.

When Queen MyrdemInggala is in need of consolation, she enters pauk, a practice not allowed by the official church. As SartoriIrvrash explains of pauk, the church "would like to ban it, but if it did so, then a million peasants would quit the Church" (*Summer*, 159).

Ironically, it is SartoriIrvrash who sets in motion the string of events that results in the demise of the Pannovalan Church. The people of Oldorando are ill prepared for his revelations that the phagors are Helliconia's senior race and that Akha is modeled in their image, remnant of an age when mankind worshipped phagors. These facts ignite the fears and doubts that underlie the population's shaky faith. Aldiss explains that SartoriIrvrash's "love of knowledge for its own sake, his hatred of his fellow men had betrayed him. He had failed to understand his audience. As a result, religious belief was set at an intolerable crisis" (*Summer*, 549). SartoriIrvrash's secluded life of study has kept him from the most basic of observations; that mankind is a social animal and that without a framework of meaning (provided, at least initially, by religion), a community can hardly cohere. His lack of knowledge in the field of relationships is parodied by the crude sexual experiments he performs on Helliconia's humanoid species, experiments that cause the death of his own wife. Billy Xiao Pin comes to terms with these issues during his brief existence on Helliconia. When initially asked about his own religious beliefs he expresses the point of view that he originally acquired aboard the Avernus:

Gods are necessary to men at some stages of development. . . I mean, as children, we need, each of us, a loving, firm, just father, to help our growth to manhood. Manhood seems to require a similar image of a father, magnified, to keep it in good check. That image bears the name of God. Only when a part of the human race grows to spiritual manhood, when it can regulate its own behaviour, does the need for gods disappear—just as we no longer need a father watching over us when we are adults and capable of looking after ourselves. (*Summer*, 244)

However, when Billy is asked if his own world, grown to manhood, is a happy one, he is forced to reflect upon his comments and realizes that his stated belief in "knowledge, certainty and control" is somehow not so firm as he thought. Billy had "escaped from a godless state to a barbaric one. And he could see, despite his own misfortunes, in which world hope of life and happiness more strongly lay" (*Summer*, 245). This idea is the essence of SartoriIrvrash's error: he fails to realize that what is needed to sustain his society is rationality tempered with compassion, that the naked truth leaves the soul unprotected from the harsh uncertainties of past and future.

These uncertainties and the events they inspire lead to the destruction of the Oldorandan palace and to the murder of the C'Sarr, representative of Akhanaba on Helliconia, by JandolAnganol's phagorian guard. As Toynbee asserts in his *Study,* the fall of a civilization is not effected by some outside agency as "the most that the alien enemy has achieved has been to give the expiring suicide his *coup de grace* or to devour his carcass after it has become carrion" (Toynbee, 6:115). JandolAnganol, despite the fact that he himself is to inherit the Oldorandan nation, recognizes the approaching twilight of his culture: "His thoughts flew to Myrdem-Inggala: but his and her summer was over, and this great bonfire of his enemies was his autumn beacon" (*Summer,* 563). This great blaze symbolizes the approaching fire of Freyr, the source of apocalyptic visions now fulfilled in both the spiritual and the physical worlds. For Freyr's approach not only terrifies the general populace but is known by the learned to cause the changing seasons. Having now reached its perihelion, Freyr recedes from Helliconia and gives way to winter, leaving the field to the civilizations that can best respond to its particular challenges. As a postscript to the Akhanaban faith in *Helliconia Winter* informs us: Akhanaba had "left the world in a pillar of flame," leaving Pannoval to become the "Country of a Thousand Cults . . . life for its inhabitants had become more uncomfortable, more uncertain" (32).

God the Azoiaxic

In *Helliconia Winter* Aldiss's attention shifts to the continent of Sibornal. Religion plays a major role in the lives of the Sibornalese, as it does on the rest of Helliconia. Through an effective merger of church and state, Sibornal has established the stability required for a civilization to endure the hardships of Helliconia's seasonal extremes. This stability has given rise to the complex association of various nations under one supreme government and church. The Sibornalese deity, God the Azoiaxic, being a more advanced spiritual form, has helped nurture humanity's more progressive tendencies. It has done so through a religion that provides spiritual health to its people through human values that encourage cooperation among nations and individuals, and hope during times of personal and environmental difficulty. This attitude is most clearly expressed through the "Great Wheel of Kharnabhar," a monumental

religious artifact built by the architects of Kharnabhar. The wheel operates through the faith and will of the Azoiaxic's followers and is constructed so as to correspond with the astronomical facts that govern
Helliconia's existence. The extent of the architects' creativity is matched
only by the power of their faith. Aldiss explains their purpose:

> They were devout men. They had believed that faith could move worlds.
> They had set about building a machine of stone which could haul Helli-
> conia across the darkness and cold until it docked again to bask in the
> warmth of God the Azoiaxic's favour. So far, the machine had always
> worked. The machine was powered by faith, and faith was in the hearts
> of men. (*Winter,* 325)

This great construction represents the essence of what religious belief
can provide. It is a metaphor that helps explain life's mysteries in a manner that rewards faith with hope. If one can experience and survive a
rotation of the wheel, then it can be understood how Helliconia can survive its orbit around Freyr. As one critic, Denise Terrel, suggests, Sibornal, home of the great wheel, is the destination of Shay Tal (spring), the
Good Hope (summer), and the New Season (winter).[21] This common
purpose suggests that the great wheel represents a spiritual ideal that is
of benefit to all the peoples of Helliconia, regardless of national boundaries.

Unfortunately, over the course of time, both the church and state of
Sibornal have become entrenched in a highly structured system that has
lost focus of the truths encompassed by the wheel. Although the Sibornalese appear to have established a form of worship that gives them
hope and relative happiness throughout the Great Year, it remains deficient with respect to the manner in which its all-too-human leaders
implement it through law and government. As with the two other Helliconian civilizations we have examined, Sibornal is a society in decline.
Not only is the Weyr winter approaching, but the repeated cycle of the
rise and fall of Sibornal's strength has induced a crisis of faith and a corresponding lack of creative energy. Sibornal's greatest achievements lay
in the past and this fact is exemplified by "The Hero," a massive statue
carved by the architects of Kharnabhar, built "many great years past" by
a "superior race of men" (*Winter,* 189). As a result Sibornal has degenerated into a land of intolerance and racism. A racial hierarchy has established itself with the Uskuti being the most privileged and the phagors
the least. Eedap Mun Odim, a Kuj Juveci, expresses his concern over
the Oligarch's many restrictive edicts: "Once more, the Uskuti were

demonstrating their racial prejudices—prejudices of which the Oligarch was quick to take advantage. Phagors had been banned from walking unattended in Sibornalese cities long ago" (*Winter*, 80).

In many ways the level of racial animosities most clearly expresses the health of a culture's spirituality, as it indicates the extent of interconnectedness among its constituent peoples. When examining the three major Helliconian religions in terms of their ability to form and/or to harmonize social units, we find that each has its own capacity for growth and a corresponding set of limitations. Belief in Wutra fostered a framework that brought individuals together to form primitive communities; Akhanaba brought communities together to form nations; God the Azoiaxic is the spiritual expression of a culture that has formed a transnational continental union. It seems that each time a religious framework is required to extend its frame of reference beyond the limits of its basic social structure, it collapses under the strain of spiritual instability. This movement can be directly related to the development of scientific knowledge and to the technological sophistication that such knowledge produces. Increasing technology allows for populations to grow through advances in agriculture, medicine, and basic tools; thus people are required to merge into larger and larger social formations. These same scientific advances, however, instill a belief in empiricism, a fascination with mere machinery, that usually conflicts with the underlying belief system. As populations grow, more advanced forms of spiritual belief are required in order to maintain the undoubted value of self-sacrificing love for others. Without such an impulse, cultural, racial, and economic differences eventually divide people and lead to self-destructive conflict, as exemplified by the war-torn "Country of a Thousand Cults," and by the increasing animosities within Sibornal itself.

For although the Sibornalese have managed to establish relatively peaceful relations among differing human cultures, they have failed to cope with the problem of the phagors. It is essential for the continued prosperity of their civilization that they respond to this challenge, since it affects Sibornalese morale and their belief in themselves as moral agents. In *Helliconia Winter* two possible solutions to the phagor challenge are considered: the first is extermination, the second involves an attempt at reconciliation. Aldiss makes clear that only reconciliation can succeed, since through a biological fluke, the "Helico" virus is necessary for human survival. Transmitted by a tick carried by the phagors, the virus metamorphoses Helliconia's humans into a body shape better suited to either winter or summer conditions. Aldiss uses this virus as an image not only to emphasize the power of biology but to suggest the need for interconnectedness among all planetary races and species. The Sibornalese attempt to reach some sort of understanding with the phagors is the chief focus of *Helliconia Winter,* which contrasts Luterin's compassionate desire to help preserve the phagor population with the Oligarch's demands for their extermination.

Lobanster Shokerandit, the Oligarch whom we discover to be Luterin's father, has lost touch with his faith and in a desperate attempt to eliminate occurrences of the "fat death" is compelled to act in a manner that may cause the end of his nation. Spurning his son's innocent optimism, he is obsessed with the apparent decline of his people, a decline he believes has been brought on by the Phagors. His scientific knowledge has deadened his faith and his moral sense, ironically undermining his rationality, so that he is prepared to eliminate the phagors even though he realizes that they are necessary for human survival. Lacking a moral grounding, the Oligarch's longing for change, the understandable need to escape from the deterministic cycle of repetition represented by the Helliconian Great Year, emerges in a negative form, as projected hate and anger. The Oligarch, for example, derides the Great Wheel, the ultimate expression of faith in God the Azoiaxic: it is an anachronism, he declares, without meaning. It functioned properly only when it supported the punishment of murderers and debtors. It is now merely an antiquated concept, one that conflicts with the scientific laws of the Oligarchy. Those laws, and those alone, the Oligarch asserts, can bring Sibornal through the Weyr-Winter. "We cannot have two sets of laws in conflict," he declares. "Therefore the Church must be demolished" (*Winter,* 317).

This erosion of faith among Sibornal's leaders creates a militaristic society whose government sees itself as superior to other cultures, especially the people of Campannlat and the phagors. The vision afforded by God the Azoiaxic of a peaceful union of peoples has become perverted by opportunism and failed faith into a view which declares that only the assimilation and purging of those who are different can ensure prosperity.

Sibornal's contact with other civilizations is shaped by an imperialist mentality. Aldiss suggests that this is the fate of a society that has enjoyed technological progress yet has lost the spiritual values that gave rise to the civilization in the first place. He creates many parallels between Sibornal and western civilization during the nineteenth- and twentieth-century age of chauvinism and technological revolution. Both these imperialist cultures (the real and the imagined) are controlled by patriarchal monologies that dominate all forms of expression. Nor does it seem inappropriate to link the Oligarch to the European fascists of the twentieth century. Lobanster Shokerandit's edicts announcing the extermination of all ancipitals and metamorphosed humans reflects the hatred that underlies unchecked racial animosities.

Without a repertory of spiritual principles to guide him, Lobanster acts out of self-interest, thus setting in motion events destined to destabilize his own imperium. The Oligarch uses the phagors to project issues of good and evil that clearly demand subtle and courageous forms of self-analysis. The Oligarch needs the phagors precisely in the way that Hitler needed the Jews and Stalin needed his purged and murdered comrades, as an imagined historical enemy to exorcise the necessity of dealing with fears relating to human mortality and failure. These historical others provide a convenient excuse for military buildup, for violence, and for murder, all in the name of a ludicrous defensiveness marshaled against the inevitable in human destiny. The slaughter of the phagors and of the transformed humans provides the Oligarch with a sense of unlimited authority and power achieved through the silencing of all opposing voices. By assuming godlike power he ceases to concern himself with dialogue. This action is, in effect, the direct opposite of what we have defined earlier as spirituality. By destroying the phagors Lobanster denies the unique bond that unites them with humans. Discussing the growth of genuine spiritual awareness, Adam Frisch and Joseph Martos note that "sooner or later, religious imagination wonders about the relationship between the inner and the outer, subject and cosmos."[22] Refusing to accept the challenge of connecting the inner and outer dimensions, failing to expand the boundaries of relationship and discourse, the Oligarch, like his real historical counterparts, becomes what the historian Burckhardt called a "terrible simplifier," asserting the rule of brute power, which leads inevitably to the ruin of the state.[23]

Earth

Despite his shrewd characterization of the Helliconia societies by means of their structures of belief, Aldiss remains a secular humanist. Far from following Toynbee in the direction of Christian revival, he makes clear that the dogma that characterizes so many organized religions often interferes with the individual's ability to understand the world in a personal and creative fashion. As Aldiss often characterizes it, custom overcomes instinct. This behavior is demonstrated throughout the *Helliconia* novels by the use of pauk as a means of spiritual expression. Pauk—a kind of private mystical experience—is neither a discovery of empirical science nor the product of a culturally dominant ideology and is vilified by both Helliconia's major churches and by the empirically minded crew of the Avernus spaceship. Neither the Helliconia nor the Avernian belief structures can accommodate experiences that do not fit established frameworks. In this way the technocentric Avernians are as much under the influence of ideological forces as are the people whom they study; in effect they have elevated the laws of science to a godlike position of authority. To be unable to accept alternative methods of understanding the universe is to be isolated from creative and regenerative ideas, as Aldiss makes clear. As Jack Voller argues, it is precisely their recognition of this fact that encourages Earth's humans to attempt empathic communication with Helliconia.[24] For them, empathy is the only means towards an even broader sense of interrelation, one that moves beyond the limitations imposed by their planet's isolation.

Toynbee argues in his *Study* that throughout history, higher religions have grown out of the encounters between different civilizations. Toynbee found that "when we mark down the birthplaces of the higher religions on a map, we find them clustering in and round two relatively small patches of the total land-surface of the Old World" (Toynbee, 8:90). A common feature of these areas is their capacity to serve as a juncture "where traffic coming in from any point of the compass could be switched to any other point of the compass in any other number of combinations" (Toynbee, 8:91). In Aldiss's imagined world, Sibornal, with access to both land and water, is described as the meeting place of Helliconia's many diverse cultures, and consequently we find that it produces Helliconia's most advanced religion. Shay Tal and Jandol-Anganol are a few among many who have traveled northward to partake in this hub of cultural activity. Koriantura, with a church dedicated to God the Azoiaxic as its central structure, is "on an important crossroads" (*Winter,* 68). It lies on the route to Campannlat, Shivennink, Carcampan, and Bribahr. These many linkages lead not only into space, but into time as well; "Koriantura was ancient and its connections with earlier ages had not been broken . . . Every lane seemed to lead backwards into time" (*Winter,* 68). Thus, Koriantura finds itself to be the home of many creative and active cultural groups, and, despite the existence of class and racial divisions, they appear to have "given it an exuberance which most cities of Sibornal did not possess, stamping that energy into its very architecture and its arts" (*Winter,* 68). This interaction among diverse cultures helps foster the essential relationships that can produce an understanding and respect for what exists beyond the narrow self. The references to tradition perhaps offer a clue to the origins of Sibornal's glorious past. As Marvin Perry defines the awareness that Sibornal is in danger of losing: "All the higher religions teach us that our wants exceed our needs, that excessive self-indulgence is an obstacle to the pursuit of spiritual aims, and that man has a moral duty to consider his neighbor's needs—attitudes which promote social progress."[25]

Sibornal, however, fails to fulfill itself as a culture, while on Earth we see achieved the fullest potential inherent in the concept of a cultural crossroads. It is on Earth, after all, that the highest civilization emerges. Voller notes that while Earth had once observed the Helliconians with detachment, Earthlings developed in time an interest in this foreign world that changed their own destiny forever.[26] Through their observations of Helliconian life, Earth's humans eventually establish an empathic contact with them. Earth becomes the meeting place for an interplanetary discourse, one that has the potential to engage all of human consciousness. This empathic contact becomes the ultimate expression of humanity's newfound sense of interconnectedness, and as Aldiss explains, it produces the very changes in mankind that Toynbee sought:

> Men and women looked about at the territory they happened to occupy and no longer asked "What can we get out of this land?" Instead they asked, "What best experience can we have on this land?" With this new consciousness came less exploitive ties and more ties everywhere, an abundance of new relationships. The ancient structure of family faded into superfamilies. All mankind became a loose-knit superorganism. (*Winter,* 247)

Thus, empathy, the ability to identify with the experiences and feelings of another, is the key to a development of a higher social order. Making use of Lovelock's Gaia theory, with its belief in a shared planetary consciousness, Aldiss is able to show that such a state of interconnectedness is indeed natural and instinctual to the human organism. Individual consciousness is given a context within which to operate by allowing for the existence of a fundamental link with the external world of nature. For David Wingrove, this is a problem that has always characterized Aldiss's fiction; the need for "apertures that look outward from the charmed circle of ritualized life into the vast wilderness of the cosmos beyond it."[27] Aldiss makes it clear that despite the possibility that exists for dialogue and the sense of belonging it fosters, there is "a lack of perfection in the scheme of things" (*Winter*, 392), and therefore, the relations we develop with the world are subject to change and decay. Despite Luterin's efforts to understand the needs of his community, he somehow falls short of expectations; there is perhaps no way for an individual ultimately to bridge the gaps that separate him from others. Luterin's final curse, his "*Abro Hakmo Astab*," shouted into the winter wind despoiling Helliconia, is both a cry of defiance and of defeat. Aldiss uses the words of the Roman poet Lucretius in his postscript to express the inevitability of change: "Everything is transformed by nature and forced into new paths. One thing, withered by time, decays and dwindles, another emerges from ignominy, and waxes strong" (*Winter*, 391).

Thus, with the near cataclysmic changes brought upon Earth by mankind's nuclear war, we witness the arrival of the geonauts, a biological entity that reveals few clues as to the ultimate purpose of its migration. The arrival, however, recapitulates the advent of human civilizations on Helliconia after the coming of Freyr. Earth's humans, however, having learned many things from their empathic contacts with Helliconia, are prepared to welcome the newcomers in a peaceful and symbiotic fashion. This peaceful relationship between humans and geonauts is symbolic of the ties that humanity has at last forged with all of nature's diversity. We are told that the geonauts are an entirely new form of life, one that exists according to principles quite different from those governing life on earth. Despite this, the human race, for once, is able to see beyond relatively narrow differences and attempts to focus on the things both species share. Even the suggestion that the geonauts will one day replace human beings is received with good will: "After all, geonauts are more beautiful and more functional than we are" (*Winter*, 347).[28]

In Aldiss's vision, this is to be Gaia's eternal legacy, that despite all of life's imperfections, we can achieve harmony within the process that is the universe. Looked at from the context of the whole *Helliconia* series, such receptivity cannot be dismissed as human fatalism; it is rather a new kind of altruism, one that reaches beyond the confines and limits of civilization and touches the cosmos itself.

With the *Helliconia* series, Brian Aldiss achieved a work far superior to most of the future histories of the postwar period. In comparison with the breadth of vision and strength of style, the depth of thought and the humanity, visible in the *Helliconia* books, comparable works by Heinlein, Asimov, and Blish seem one-dimensional, superficial, or merely entertaining. Aldiss's only real rival—and the model he had in mind—is clearly Olaf Stapledon's *Last and First Men.* Both of these impressive books have their bleak sides, but the *Helliconia* series is more of a fiction and less of a chronicle than the earlier work. It is balanced, powerful, and keeps the human in scale with the cosmic. There is little doubt that the *Helliconia* series is Brian Aldiss's most impressive work of science fiction.

Chapter Four

Literary Games:
Aldiss's Experimental and
Intertextual Fiction

Literature is a game with tacit conventions; to violate them partially or totally is one
of the many joys (one of the many obligations) of the game, whose limits are
unknown.

—Jorge Luis Borges, *Other Inquisitions* (1964)

Throughout his life Brian Aldiss has been an omnivorous reader, an
exceptionally gifted conversationalist and parodist, as well as an imaginative critic of all kinds of literature. In 1988 he even became a stage
performer, touring in England and Germany with "Science Fiction
Blues: The Show that Brian Aldiss Took on the Road." After hearing one
of his public conversations at a Florida fantasy convention in 1989,
Doris Lessing wrote: "I didn't want to miss a single word, I didn't want
it to end. But alas at last it did and Brian said what a treat it was for
him, how few people could do this—could match him, I *think* he said,
and he might even have breathed that it was a sad thing to own a
Stradivarius and be so seldom able to use it. It is a Stradivarius all
right."[1]

Aldiss's gift for literary games, his sharp intelligence, and his delight
in so many kinds of literature made it almost certain that he would end
up writing the kind of fiction that plays on other fiction, works of wit
and allusion that push and stretch the language, fiction that challenges
the assumptions of conventional narrative. Pastiche and parody, intertextual romps, takeoffs, and inversions appear everywhere in the Aldiss
canon. Broadly speaking, however, we may divide his works in this vein
into three categories: parody (*The Saliva Tree* and some of *The Eighty
Minute Hour*); intertextual game-playing (*Frankenstein Unbound, Dracula
Unbound,* and *Moreau's Other Island*); and his own versions of modernist

experiments with fictional narrative (*Report on Probability A, Barefoot in the Head, Brothers of the Head,* and *An Age*).

The Saliva Tree

The Saliva Tree (1965), an inspired pastiche based on the work of H. G. Wells, won the Nebula Award as the best science fiction novella of 1965.[2] Like most such parodistic works, this takeoff depends greatly for its effect on the reader's knowledge of the originals.

The action is set in a sleepy East Anglian farming community at the end of the nineteenth century. We learn that a gifted new writer, Mr. H. G. Wells, has just published a book called *The Time Machine*. Wells himself is an offstage character; on the very last page of Aldiss's story the great man arrives to meet the protagonist Gregory Rolles, an admirer of his, who, will clearly be able to deliver to "H.G." enough material to keep him busy at his writing desk for several years!

Like the early stories of Wells, *The Saliva Tree* begins in an almost comically parochial local environment but quickly evokes cosmic reflections and connections.[3] Gregory Rolles and his friend Bruce Fox observe what they think is a meteor strike the earth on a nearby farm. The next day Rolles visits the place, and we are introduced to Joseph Grendon, the farmer, his wife, his pretty daughter Nancy, and the two hired men, Bert and Grubby. The "meteor" has actually crashed into the Grendon pond, and when Rolles explores the pond alone, his small raft is nearly upset by an invisible and seemingly malicious force. He convinces himself that he has imagined this, but stranger things follow: an ill-smelling mist descends on the farm; crops grow at an incredible rate, yet the produce that results seems to have a bad taste. Young Rolles, a devoted fan of H. G. Wells, who corresponds with the great man, finally realizes that aliens have landed and are taking over the place. Since the supposed meteor appeared to materialize from the constellation Auriga, Rolles decides that the visitors are Aurigans.

The story goes rollicking on, building from absurdity to absurdity: the farm becomes extremely dangerous, yet old Grendon's greed prevents him from leaving, despite the weird happenings; he has never had such profitable crops and such a multiplication of livestock. "I got this here farm, you see, and I'm the farm and it is me." After a comical fight with Bert over Nancy, Rolles's observations lead him to decide that the Aurigans are using the farm to produce food for themselves. Why have they come to earth? He isn't sure, but Nancy suggests that they may just be on vacation, or on a honeymoon—"same as we might go to Great Yarmouth for a couple of days for our honeymoon"—and of course they would have to eat. Crazy things happen: Mrs. Grendon gives birth to nine children and suffocates them rather than go insane from their demands. (She goes insane anyway and is eaten by the Aurigans.) A number of pitched battles are fought against the invisible aliens—Rolles dusts them with flour and discovers that they are monsters ten to twelve feet tall, with multiple limbs sprouting from the tops of their heads. The Aurigans eat their prey by injecting them with a venom that dissolves bodily organs, after which they suck out the jelly, leaving only a deflated carapace of skin behind. In turn, many of the farm animals, the farmhand Grubby, and finally the indomitable farmer himself are consumed by the invaders.

Gregory Rolles (whose vaguely socialistic and benevolent regard for all living things has been sorely tested) dreams of a metallic tree that eats people ("the saliva tree"). This dream or nightmare, in which Gregory finds himself embracing Nancy, only to see her face dissolve when he touches it with tree-saliva, seems to parallel Victor Frankenstein's guilty dream of his mother and Elizabeth in Mary Shelley's novel more than it does anything in Wells. It also seems to take the novella into a rather too serious realm at the wrong moment.[4] Nonetheless, the inspired farce resumes and although Nancy hesitates to leave her father, she is eventually dragged off the farm by Gregory.

By this time, everything has been reduced to a chaos almost beyond description, and the farm is a huge blaze (fires are a commonplace in Wells, as V. S. Pritchett once observed), but Gregory has impressed his Nancy by managing to wound one of the Aurigans. Gregory has also been wise enough to get in touch with his friend H. G. Wells, who comes all the way from Worcester Park, Surrey, to investigate. Wells never quite enters the story—and in any case he is too late to catch the action: the farm is gone, and the Aurigans have taken off for wherever. The reader suspects, however, that this may not prevent the great man from profiting by the trip!

The Saliva Tree, apart from the title and Gregory's odd dream, which skew the reader's attention somewhat, is a remarkable piece of work, one based on a detailed knowledge of Wells's style as well as his plots and themes. Aldiss "fakes" a leisured, late Victorian, labored narrative that is eerily evocative of the master. He gives just the right twist of absurdity to the link between the local and the cosmic that is so striking in Wells and creates cannibalistic monsters to rival those in *The War of the Worlds.* He mimics themes and images in "A Story of Days to Come," *The Food of the Gods, The Invisible Man,* and many other famous Wells stories. He captures the spirit of Wellsian farce and faithfully reproduces the typically rather ponderous and hesitant Wells hero, who is surrounded in turn by characters so unbudging in their conventional views that almost no cosmic calamity can shock them into a new vision. Like all good parodies, Aldiss's story derives its comedy from the limitations of literary gesture implicit in the familiar original texts.[5] Thanks to Aldiss, we magically reacquaint ourselves with Wells's style and themes and recognize and enjoy them as part of an already assimilated literary history. We are able to laugh at our own once credulous acceptance of these texts and to reexperience them from a more sophisticated angle.

The Saliva Tree will no doubt have a permanent place, along with Kurt Vonnegut's *The Sirens of Titan* and other works in the science fiction canon of inspired spoofs. Of course it is difficult to guess how the story would be judged by a reader unfamiliar with the Wellsian reference points—perhaps as a rather curious East Anglian successor to *Cold Comfort Farm.* The comparison is fair enough. Stella Gibbons produced her parody not merely out of malice but out of lingering affection for the often portentous west-country world created in the fiction of Thomas Hardy, the Powys brothers, and Mary Webb. In *The Saliva Tree* Aldiss recalls with amusement and obvious delight the innocent Wells stories, especially those that lie closest to his own East Anglian roots. *The Saliva Tree* is a more genial and less challenging kind of playing with literature than Aldiss was to attempt in his later works, yet it is almost entirely successful, which can hardly be said for all of them. In *The Saliva Tree* Aldiss found an amusing way of using intertextuality, of playing the literary game, but his next attempts at this kind of fiction changed the stakes quite considerably.

Report on Probability A

Report on Probability A, written in 1962, was at first rejected by Aldiss's publisher Faber & Faber.[6] No doubt the strictures of conservative litterateurs such as novelist-scientist C. P. Snow, who often railed in print and in person against the tediums of the French *nouveau roman,* worked against the book. Aldiss writes that he was "much persuaded by the French *nouveau roman,* the anti-novel, as practiced by Michel Butor and Alain Robbe-Grillet . . . I admired their scrapping of many literary cliches . . . I was stunned by the Robbe-Grillet-Resnais film, *L'Annee*

Derniere a Marienbad, with its temporal confusions, mysterious agonies, and alien perspectives. It still embodies for me many of the things I set most store by in SF."[7]

By the time Faber & Faber did publish *Report* in 1968, the resistance against Robbe-Grillet and the other antinovelists, chroniclers of seemingly disconnected particularities, had softened. At the same time, the heady elixir of the new wave was being distributed, almost as a sacramental brew, to an unwilling science fiction fandom. "You have never read a book like this before, and the next time you read one anything like it, it won't be *much* like it at all," wrote Judith Merril, in her introduction to *England Swings SF,* an anthology that brought the British new wave to American readers.[8] In the same book she prints a surrealistic interview with Aldiss in which he protests that the new wave is really not new and not very interesting; he does not say so, but clearly he had other literary goals in mind, ambitions to bring the *nouveau roman* to British fiction. Yet the fact that Michael Moorcock was willing to publish such a grimly determined piece of experimental fiction as *Report on Probability A* in his magazine *New Worlds* showed how far science fiction had moved away not only from the pulps but from its postwar fusions with mainstream fiction.[9] And an audience of sorts did exist. Paperback editions of *Report* followed and the novel received some favorable notices from informed critics.[10]

Even so, reading the text from the perspective of the 1990s, one is inclined to side with the skeptics. *Report on Probability A* is an exercise in the static. The narrative focuses on principal characters known only by their initials; they spend all their time watching each other: G, S, and C watch Mr. and Mrs. Mary, while they watch G, S, and C. Many scenes are described in detail, but narrative thrust is virtually absent, exactly as Aldiss intended. Aldiss's approach throughout is clinically objective and lacking in drama, climax, or emotional commitment. "I withhold the emotions involved, so that the reader must put in emotion for himself," he wrote.[11] There are many repeated passages and no plot; the book plays no allusive literary game: nor is the reader given the satisfaction of solving an intellectual puzzle. Nothing happens, nothing is explained, and there is no conclusion; nor does the fixation on detail lift the reader into a vision of the strangeness of the ordinary, as in the best of magic realism.

One of the key images of the book is William Holman Hunt's Pre-Raphaelite painting "The Hireling Shepherd," which seems to exist in a curious temporal nexus visible from each character's otherwise solipsistic perspective.[12] The painting itself, we are told, is an example of "imprisonment of beings in a temporal structure"—which seems to be precisely the effect that Aldiss strives to show in this novel.[13] Unfortunately, he seems to forget that the Holman Hunt painting, whatever "static" might mean as applied to it, has both brilliant color that stimulates the eye and a subject that arouses the voyeurism of the viewer in a way that his own narrative does not. Novels are not paintings—they are structures of words unfolded by the reader in his or her own time—and to eliminate duration from the novel is nearly as unthinkable as eliminating it from music. "All we are after is fact. We don't have to decide what reality is, thank God!" says one of the characters. The novelist, however, does, and the epigraph from Goethe—"Do not, I beg you, look for anything behind phenomena. They are themselves their own lesson"—is clearly an injunction directed at philosophical idealism of a certain kind and not an invitation to the fiction writer to attempt to freeze time and disintegrate meaning into discrete and distanced perceptions.[14] J. G. Ballard seems to locate the book's main problem when he argues that *Report* fossilizes events so completely that the reader's brain is paralyzed, thus breaking "the vital link in this or any other chain of perception—that between the book and its reader."[15] Aldiss continues to defend the book, considering it an artistic success because he achieved what he set out to do, but the unentertained reader may be driven to recall the precept of Jules Renard, who reminded us that "art is no excuse for boring people."[16]

An Age

Published in 1967, *An Age* (published in the United States as *Cryptozoic,* 1968) was written after *Report on Probability A,* and is therefore the second in order of Aldiss's highly experimental 1960s trio of "anti-sciencefiction" novels.[17] It is in many ways a transition book, for it reveals a great deal of stylistic diversity and perhaps too much uncertainty of mood and focus. While the reader senses the book's importance, he or she may find it flawed in conception and execution. Undeniably, however, it moves Aldiss out of the impasse created by *Report* and by *Barefoot in the Head* and points the way, for better or worse, to both *Frankenstein Unbound* and *The Eighty-Minute Hour.*

   An Age is first of all a novel about time and was dubbed by Aldiss as a "landscape with surrealism," leading Richard Matthews to connect it with Salvador Dali's famous surrealistic painting "The Persistence of

Memory."[18] The novel extrapolates social escapism into the year 2093, when a mind-altering drug known as CSD allows a form of time travel that is really a mental voyage, one that does not allow the time-traveler to affect the physical reality of the worlds visited. So many citizens indulge in this travel, however, that the economy collapses and England is taken over by a totalitarian regime. The book's protagonist, Edward Bush, a played-out sculptor, is brutally compelled by the regime to pursue Silverstone, a speculative thinker who knows the secret of time and is hiding in the far past. Bush has already traveled far back and met a woman, Ann, who is a guide-mentor figure, a kind of anima, on whose name Aldiss puns freely in the book's title and elsewhere. On his new mission Bush lands first in the 1930s and witnesses a family tragedy precipitated by a coal-mining strike, one that fills him with grief at his own hitherto selfish existence. He decides to save Silverstone, and they flee together with two others to the Jurassic Age, where Silverstone reveals to Eddie the secret of time, which is, that it actually flows backwards. Humans invented a reverse time in the Stone Age to escape from the intolerable notion of incest. We actually travel, not from womb to tomb but on the reverse path; what we think of as ancient history, the past, is really our future—thus memory is really prophecy and prophecy memory. This thought is most comforting to Eddie Bush, whose Oedipal longings have been well displayed by Aldiss from the beginning of this tale. As the novel ends, we are back in the year 2093. Eddie Bush's father goes to the Carlfield Advanced Mental Disturbances Institution to inquire about his son, who has been incarcerated as a lunatic. Is the whole story of travel to the Jurassic, then, just the ravings of a madman? Or is the mysterious and perhaps potent Ann really watching the institution, as she seems to be, and preparing to rescue Eddie Bush, as part of a metaplot that will carry him once again away from the imprisonment in the present that seems to be the worst fate of the year 2093 (or of any year?).[19]

In *An Age*, "the persistence of memory," refers then to a supposed future time, which is really the past, and so justifies science fiction, not as prophecy, but as historical re-creation. Aldiss's inversion in an ingenious manner moves him away from the entropic "dead end" of *Report on Probability A;* at the same time, the dystopian chaos of *Barefoot in the Head* is potentially transcended. Characteristically, the science fiction writer explores an imagined future as a way of illuminating or defining the present. Such a writer is in a sense sculpting with time, and it is not difficult to see that *An Age,* with its artist protagonist, is also a novel about the power of imagination in the present, a novel about the artist's, the science fiction writer's, potentialities and options. Can the writer's imaginative projections—scorned by some—say anything about our present reality? Is Eddie Bush merely deluded? The book tracks the path from narcissism and obsession to potential communication, if not to hope. Not only does it reinforce Aldiss's commitment to his science fiction perspective; it also sets the terms of his next few experimental novels, at least two of which move back to the question of intertextuality raised in *The Saliva Tree*. Time, too, becomes a central issue in the next books, and Aldiss increasingly treats it as a pressure on our world, as the most brutally operative of human abstractions, and as a potential vehicle of clarification.

Barefoot in the Head: A European Fantasia

Following on this ingenious exercise, Aldiss produced another puzzling fiction, but one of a very different character. He took up the line of Joyce and Samuel Beckett, fashioning a verbal extravaganza that attempted to break the conventions of the novel, not by sinking it into a timeless entropy, or by disrupting the narrative with odd leaps to almost unimaginable time periods, but by exploding the verbal line to render the psychedelic furor of the sixties and by linking the plot, albeit ironically, to the idea of awakening espoused by the philosopher-mystic George Ivanovitch Guardieff.[20]

Barefoot in the Head: A European Fantasia (1969) takes place after an "acid head" war, one that has figuratively blown the brains of most of the population of Europe. The protagonist Colin Charteris, a Yugoslavian named after the popular novelist Leslie Charteris, drives across the continent and Aldiss gives his journey a punning and parodistic connection with the conception of "man the driver," Guardieff's image of the human self operating under the illusion of personal freedom. The Europe Charteris encounters ("charts" is a key word, as Richard Matthews assures us) is disintegrating; its veil of reality ripped apart, and as he travels through it, his own mind begins to fracture into conceptions diverse and unreconcilable.[21] Charteris, although he degenerates into a megalomaniac murderer and a schizoid opportunist, eventually gathers a following and becomes a kind of Timothy Leary cum Charles Manson pseudosavior. A film on Charteris is planned, one that will feature multiple car crashes and real deaths (shades of J. G. Ballard!). This film, however, is destroyed in the spreading social chaos, and

Charteris is eventually incarcerated in a mental hospital run by a Herr Laundrei, a sadistic exaggeration of the misguided therapist sardonically implied in the writings of the famous sixties "anti-therapist" R. D. Laing. The book dissolves in a series of surrealistic fugues originating from and surrounding the main character and concludes with a barrage of ragged, off-the-wall poetry.

The world recorded in this book is a nightmarish extrapolation from the sixties; on the one hand mechanical contrivances dominate everything, the car is king and the superhighway is the artery of connection between meaningless part and part.[22] At the same time communication has degenerated into the equality and incomprehension of Babel: art, religion, politics, economics, and popular culture jostle together in the ironical Utopia ("nowhere") of mass society. In this swamp of meaninglessness and motion, mystical conceptions and delusions flourish like grotesque plants. While in the Yeatsian sense, "things fall apart, the centre cannot hold, mere anarchy is loosed upon the world," spiritual megalomania is rampant and multifaceted, since as Guardieff's conception has it, everyone is a multitude of selves without a center but with the fatal illusion of control. The quest for reality is doomed to end up in an almost infinite number of blind alleys.

The language of *Barefoot in the Head* is at one with the tenor of the story: as the protagonist's mind disintegrates, the conventional patterns of grammar and syntax are collapsed into a verbal fabric replete with multiple puns and allusions and plays on words, very much in the fashion of *Finnegan's Wake*. The mythos, or narrative structure, on the other hand, fractures into multiple pathways without any privileged direction. The Joycean punning, however, grows wearisome to many readers; narrowness rather than breadth results because the language in its endless allusiveness splinters the meaning into too many isolated bits. And though a single unifying voice underlies the diversity, it too much resembles that of a clever undergraduate, self-consciously delivering a surrealistic monologue at the climax of some rowdy midnight party.

> All untold the fey atmosfuddle of selforiented libidoting wooze trixfixed the constabulary into poets longhaired boxers instrumentalists vocalists meditationers on a semi-syllable card trick-exponents voyeurs of the world box word-munchering followsphere semi-lovers of course with the greatest pretentions wrackonteurs charmers butchboys frenchmen twotkissing mystics like-feathered nestlings vanvogtian autobiographers laughers chucklers starers stargazers villagers and simple heart-burglars all seeing themselves shining in their hip-packet mirrors.[23]

In such passages, for all their burden of sheer cleverness, a sympathetic critic might note that Aldiss was not merely following Joyce, but also anticipating later developments, new perspectives in science and art, for to extrapolate endlessly from a pun or play on words is to begin to fractilize reality in the manner described by chaos theory.[24] At many points in *Barefoot in the Head* one statement or event leads directly, although almost randomly, to the next, like the multiplication of lines in a Mandelbrot figure, even though an overarching meaning, or final resolution, is missing.[25] The result is a patterning that has an irregular beauty, but one that is literally without boundaries (the novel doesn't "end"; it merely peters out). Throughout, language is used to demonstrate the potency of "strange attractors," forms that cling together, underlying and defining chaos without actually suggesting the patterns of a higher order.[26]

Questions remain, however. How does such a fiction relate to the typical reader's sense of what a novel should be? How does it relate to science fiction? First, *Barefoot in the Head* is clearly a more intriguing and engaging novel than its inert twin, *Report on Probability A,* for while *Barefoot* is admittedly often baffling, it does capture (however crazily and fleetingly) many kinds of reality and offers the pleasures of the language game in a way that *Report on Probability A* does not. Thus, the novel invites us to "dope out" its difficult passages, to place them in the literary-cultural context defined by Joyce and Beckett. In doing so we may be convinced that we are making sometimes cogent links to the real world culture of the 1960s, and even to our present world, one equally resonant with absurdly incompatible elements and possessing scientific notions (chaos theory) that may be fruitfully applied to the novel. *Barefoot in the Head* tends toward the static only in the sense that the fractilizing of language may slow the reader down; on the whole the narrative evokes a chaos that is full of infinite possibilities. In this work Aldiss carries the Joyce-derived novel in the direction of postmodern trends such as indeterminacy, selflessness, unrepresentation, and carnivalization—to use the terms of Ihab Hassan.[27] At the level of genre, it can be argued that *Barefoot in the Head* combines dystopia with fantasy, quest narrative with satire: and if this constitutes an unpalatable mixture for the common reader of science fiction, that is exactly what Aldiss expected and strove for. "It took me almost three years to write," he commented later, "and when I'd finished it, I felt I'd written myself out of SF."[28]

In fact, immediately after the appearance of *Barefoot in the Head,* Aldiss began to bring out the first books of his Horatio Stubbs trilogy, in which the literary high jinks and high spirits that characterize *Barefoot* took quite another form (see chapter 5). It was not until 1973 that he published another science fiction novel, *Frankenstein Unbound,* a popular work that picks up on the game of allusion begun in *The Saliva Tree* and attempts to carry it to a deeper dimension.

Frankenstein Unbound

In *Frankenstein Unbound,* the hero Joe Bodenland, who lives in 2020 A.D., enters a time rift and arrives in Switzerland in 1816, driving a well-armed nuclear-powered car. To his surprise, he meets Victor Frankenstein and soon attends the trial of Justine Moritz for the murder of Frankenstein's brother William. She is condemned to death; Bodenland follows Victor up to the hills and catches a glimpse of the Frankenstein monster. Bit by bit he recalls events from the Frankenstein story. Attempting to save Justine, he seeks out the creator of the Frankenstein story at the Villa Diodati complex on Lac Leman. But time rifts again occur and he gets there, it appears, in the fall, after Justine has been executed. At the villa he meets first Lord Byron, then Shelley, and finally Mary Wollstonecraft (as he is careful to call her). Bodenland seems to forget his mission while he discusses the future of western society with the poets—he is trying to remember the story of Frankenstein and attempting to figure out why both real historical people and the characters of the novel seem to exist on the same level of reality, something the reader may be puzzled by as well. While the men are away, Bodenland, alone with Mary Shelley, tries to explain the situation to her. After a nude swim and some preliminary flirting, they promptly go to bed. She explains that she hasn't yet finished writing her famous novel, but when he reveals his origins in the far future, and tells her about his encounter with the monster and Frankenstein, she accepts his story with surprising ease. Although puzzled and upset, Mary accompanies him to the car, and he leaves in pursuit of the monster. He goes back to Geneva, visits the Frankenstein house and, after an unfriendly meeting with Elisabeth and Clerval (no convincing reason is given for their hostility), he is pursued and arrested by the police (considering the absence of any telephones, the reader is left wondering how the police happened to be summoned so conveniently from the house). Bodenland is thrown into jail, where he writes an embarrassingly silly letter to Mary Godwin.

> What I will write about is the world situation in which I find myself. I bless you that you are an intellectual girl, like your mother, in an age when such spirits are rare; in my age they are less rare, but perhaps no more effectual because of their greater numbers, and because they operate in a world where the male principle has prevailed, even over the mentalities of many of your sex. (I'd say all this differently in the language of my time! Would you like to hear it? You are an early example of Women's Lib, baby, just like your Mom. Your cause will grab more power as time passes, boosted by the media, who always love a new slant on the sex thing. But most of those fighting girls have sold themselves out to the big operators, and work the male kick themselves, clitoris or no clitoris . . .)[29]

Bodenland's summary of social changes here and elsewhere in this letter seems to serve no dramatic purpose; the superficiality of its arguments, as well as the calculated and vulgarly obvious slip into twentieth-century jargon (by a narrator who is supposed to come from the twenty-first century!), is likely to cause the reader to wonder about Aldiss's overall control of his stylistics. Narrative implausibilities multiply: a great flood frees Bodenland from the prison; he finds that a warp in time and space has disfigured the landscape of the Geneva region. He flees to the hills and survives, thanks to a gift of food from the Frankenstein monster. He returns to Geneva, insists on seeing Frankenstein, and is taken to Victor's tower-laboratory. He manages to drug Victor and inspects the laboratory, where a mate is being prepared for the monster (she wears the face of Justine). In chapter 19 Aldiss achieves a brief moment of narrative integrity as Bodenland passionately questions his previous naive adherence to the values of science and progress:

> Organized religion, indeed! What had we in its place? Organized science! Whereas organized religion was never well organized, and often ran contrary to commercial interests, it had been forced to pay lip service, if not more than that, to the idea that there was a place in the scheme of things for the least among us. But organized science had allied itself with Big Business and Government; it had no interest in the individual—its meat was statistics! It was death to the spirit. (*Unbound*, 171)

This lament for lost values is unusual in Aldiss's work, as is the specific plea on behalf of religion and the directness of the attack on science; unfortunately, in the melodramatic context of the narrative, the rhetoric seems arbitrary and unmotivated. Nonetheless, it marks a last moment of intellectual integrity in this text, which thereafter collapses into B-movie absurdity. Bodenland recovers his futuristic car, which has been obligingly deposited behind Frankenstein's tower. Justifying his actions by the most dubious and one-sided arguments, Bodenland then murders Victor, the monster, and his newly animated mate—the latter two after a chase into the far north, which seems to have been inserted only so as to allow Aldiss to conclude the novel with the phrase "darkness and distance," the very words Mary Shelley used to end her own text.

Several of Aldiss's reputable critics have written extensively about *Frankenstein Unbound,* treating the book as if its implicit ideas, and their exegesis, were in fact realized in the text.[30] More to the point is the comment of Dan Miller: "Ted White, writing in the Chicago Literary Review, had this to say about the book: 'It's a dreadfully bad novel, badly plotted, badly written, badly conceived. The characterizations are absurd throughout . . . all are doom-driven pieces of cardboard.' This is a charitable assessment of the book."[31] Miller and White are surely correct: *Frankenstein Unbound* is one of Aldiss's large literary failures.

The novel disappoints in many ways. For one thing, the main character, Joe Bodenland, has no psychic weight—his inner life and emotions seem stunted, and the reader doesn't for a minute believe in him or care about him. Bodenland leaves the future, his wife, and his children, and thereafter hardly gives them a thought. His trip through time is badly rendered. Aldiss muffs small, and not so small, details of plot. When Bodenland arrives he does business at a Swiss inn and rents a boat, but there is no explanation of where he got the money to do this. Immediately afterward, however, he pawns his watch in order to get money to operate in the Swiss society of 1816, thus calling the reader's attention to the initial gaffe. The poets Byron and Shelley appear as shallow caricatures—which may irritate the knowing reader, who will mentally be comparing the gabble of Aldiss's Byron with the poet's brilliant letters. Even worse, as Aldiss tells it, Mary Shelley gets the origin of her famous novel wrong. She claims that *Frankenstein* was inspired by a dream, whereas her 1831 preface describes it as being derived from a hypnagogic state preceding sleep.[32] The notion that the severe and somewhat straitlaced Mary, Shelley's "cold chaste moon," would jump into bed with a stranger she is meeting for almost the first time might be acceptable to a *Playboy* audience in the mid-1970s but it lacks historical or narrative plausibility. Aldiss makes Mary's acceptance of the time-traveling Bodenland and his story about his past and her own future far too easy. Her behavior in these scenes, if we can take her character seriously at all, is as flippantly false as the behavior of Francis Ford Coppola's Victorian women in his film version of Bram Stoker's *Dracula*.

Frankenstein Unbound found the appropriate moviemaker in Roger Corman, an erratic but sometimes interesting low-budget director, whose film version of the text was released in 1990.[33] Put bluntly, it might be said that, in terms of structure, style, and depth of focus, *Frankenstein Unbound* is a distinctly low-budget Brian Aldiss novel.

The Eighty-Minute Hour

The Eighty-Minute Hour, published in 1974, is, on the other hand, one of Brian Aldiss's most successful experiments. It is a work of dazzling stylistics, an intricately structured intellectual comedy that never descends into mere frivolity.

The setting is the earth and the solar system up until about 1999, but there are glimpses of the far past and of the far future; numerous characters weave in and out of the narrative, important themes are raised, dropped, and then reappear in a new perspective. The narrative is fragmented so as to capture the space time distortions recounted in the story: characters who at first glance seem unconnected cross paths, while the first-person storyteller Durrant hardly upsets the reader's sense of a third-person narrative. In all of this, the heady worlds of Philip K. Dick and Kurt Vonnegut are not far away. Aldiss's admiration for the former, in particular, has never been in doubt, and while this novel can hardly be read as merely another Aldiss parody, it is full of the kind of wild plot shifting that Dick manages with such ease. At the same time, the intellectually dazzling game Aldiss manages with space-time concepts and robotics recalls the work of Italo Calvino (the *Cosmicomics*, for example), while the tone of the comedy and the interplay of characters is not far in spirit from Thomas Pynchon. In short, *The Eighty-Minute Hour* is one of those works that brings science fiction and postmodernism into close relationship.[34]

The novel describes an earth radically changed by a major global nuclear war. England has sunk beneath the sea; the moon has been destroyed and the fabric of the universe itself has been altered. Space-time disturbances begin to appear in the year 1999, the product of the immense heat produced by nuclear detonations (1000 times the temperature of the sun), and so humanity is faced with a new, unexpected form of pollution. As well, advanced computer technologies have made new forms of spatial existence possible (microspace), which effectively disrupts humankind's notion of nature and existence. The global nuclear war also induced the restructuring of political alignments. In the year 1996 the Cap-Comm (capitalist-communist) merger was struck. This alliance effectively united the world's major powers into a single, more efficient entity. Attica Saigon Smix is the president of Cap-Comm and head of the World Executive Council. The corporate branch of Cap-Comm is called Smix-Smith, named after Attica Saigon Smix and its companalog (or super computer), John Thunderbird Smith. This corporation is responsible for the implementation of efficiency in all of mankind's endeavors, as symbolized by Computer Complex's attempt to implement an eighty-minute hour. Opposed to Cap-Comm are the Idealists of the Decadent Id (IDI), a Marxist group led by Mike Surinat.

IDI fears the fanatical implementation of efficiency and the work plus deadly monotony that it creates.[35] As George Hornbeck, Mike Surinat's mentor, states: "I believe work is mankind's worst vice and affliction, killing more people year after year than all your drugs and automobiles combined. Even worse, it exhausts the planet as well as mankind . . . order and progress lead to war" (*Hour,* 14).

The plot itself revolves around the search for three missing persons; Attica Saigon Smix, Auden Chaplain, and Choggles Chaplain. The disappearance of the 10-year-old girl, Choggles Chaplain, occurs at a party in the castle of Slavonski Brod that belongs to Mike Surinat, cousin of Choggles, founder of the IDI, and a diplomat for the Dissident Nations, an alliance that opposes Cap-Comm. This party is used as a setting to introduce a large number of characters as well as to explain their various political affiliations. Choggles is not with her parents. Her father Auden Chaplain is infamous for creating a device, the Schally-Chaplain switch, which was implanted in every human skull to enforce Cap-Comm's policy of zero population growth. Auden has not been seen for many years and rumors circulate that he fled to the Martian colonies in fear of an attempt on his life, although most believe he is already dead. Those individuals attending Mike's party by and large support the Dissident Nations, including the perceptive Becky Hornbeck and the glamorous and famous Glamis Fevertrees. Only two guests, old friends of Mike, support the Cap-Comm merger: Sue Fox, a member of the World Executive Council, and Monty Zoomer, a famous pop star whose holodreams have made him a celebrity. Monty is in the employment of Cap-Comm as an official supplier of holodreams; in reality it is Attica Saigon Smix who uses Zoomer as part of his propaganda campaign to keep Cap-Comm in power. Zoomer wears around his neck a pendant that Smix has given him and told him to protect. Taken with the charms of Glamis Fevertrees, Zoomer attempts to seduce her. Glamis is flirtatious in return but cites the fact that her sister Loomis is married to Zoomer's boss Smix as a possible complication. With a dramatic gesture, Zoomer offers his pendant to Glamis as a token of his love and Glamis, already covetous of this beautiful Martian-made trinket, accepts it willingly and gives Zoomer her own, somewhat less beautiful pendant. Zoomer then attends to his assigned task. Creating a hologram of Choggles' mother Leda, he convinces Choggles that her father Auden is alive and awaiting her on Mars. Anxious to see her father again, she enters a car with the Holman who drives her out to Zoomer's flying machine; she recognizes it as such, but it is too late for her to escape.

After the party Glamis takes part in an important mission for the Dissident Nations, surveying the shipping routes near Jupiter. It is here aboard the spaceship Doomwitch that the time disturbances begin to appear. Doomwitch disappears, Jupiter vanishes. Back on Earth, the World Executive Council is in session attempting to make order of an increasingly chaotic situation. As Smix himself states, "we must now face up to the fact that more than one time can exist simultaneously" (*Hour,* 71). The council reports that a whole section of South Africa has slipped back into 1879 and that Zulu tribes are attacking. Russian troops are attacking the Ottoman army outside of Adrianople. Britain has invaded Afghanistan. For the companalog John Thunderbird Smith, these unpredictable occurrences are too much: "These anomalies in the functioning of the natural order cannot be tolerated," he announces (*Hour,* 72).

Meanwhile Attica, we discover, is hidden in a "bolt-hole," a form of microspace aboard the spaceship Micromegas. In case this concept is not clear to the reader, Aldiss allows the ship's Captain Ladore some wonderful lines of "explanation":

> This aponeurotic floor is maintained in stasis by a power-drain from some of the newly-opened-up universes. The energy quotients appear to be in equipoise, so that one year of the floor's existence probably drains one year from the entropaic-output store of an entire universe. (*Hour,* 28)

Attica has in fact chosen to hide out in the pendant he had given to Monty Zoomer. When a signal is given, the Micromegas is designed to home in on this pendant and thus spring Attica from the bolt-hole.

Unfortunately for him, the unreliable Monty Zoomer has given away the pendant to Glamis, who has traveled back in time aboard the Doomwitch. The Doomwitch and its crew have regressed more than 2000 years into the past, to the time of Plato, a time with no landing spaces adequate to land the Doomwitch! Unknowingly, Smix is as much trapped in the past as is the Doomwitch crew. Glamis, in a desperate attempt to seek help from the future that has been left behind, sends out a message to her old lover Jack Dagenfort. Dagenfort is an idealist who once was an assistant on Auden Chaplain's zero population growth project, though he later repented of this technology and joined the forces of IDI. Jack makes contact with Per Gilleleje, operations chief at IDI headquarters, to find that they are also seeking to contact him.

Per reassures Dagenfort that they will attempt to retrieve Glamis and the Doomwitch and informs Jack that Choggles Chaplain has been abducted and that it is believed that Auden is alive and working in the Martian colonies. In league with Attica Smix, Auden and his technological knowledge could be extremely dangerous to the Dissident Nations. As Jack Dagenfort is one of the few people who could recognize Auden, he is asked to fly to Mars and apprehend him and perhaps locate the young Choggles as well. In fact, Choggles has been taken by the dopple (similitude) of her mother to the Godwin Universal Holodreams Studios where Monty Zoomer works. To make things almost unbearably complicated, the Holodreams Studios are hit by a time disturbance before we find out what Choggles' fate was to be.

A bare summary can only hint at the high jinks that follow, although these center on two quests. The first is Thunderbird Smith's attempt to locate Attica Saigon Smix, who has fled his post in order to escape his enemies and to keep Cap-Comm at its maximum (nonhuman) efficiency. The other quest is Jack Dagenfort's attempt to find Auden Chaplain on Mars. The exchanged pendants, however, interfere with the Thunderbird Smith computer's search, in particular when Smix, Glamis, and the crew of the Doomwitch are catapulted through a time-space disturbance five billion years into the past. When Glamis and Jules de l'Isle-Evens, a Cap-Comm scientist, awaken from a slumber, they find themselves on a strange planet, described in some detail by Aldiss. Aboard the Micromegas, Attica Smix is no longer picking up any signals from outside his bolt hole, since he, of course, has been sent back in time along with the Doomwitch. He is afraid that Computer Complex has discovered his secret and thus emerges from microspace, only to find himself on a strange new planet, now named Glamis. He explains that the forces of Computer Complex are after him; now Glamis and Jules realize that if the forces of Cap-Comm led by Thunderbird Smith should appear, their rocket thrusters could easily ignite the planet's vast store of hydrogen. While Saigon Smix is occupied, they steal the Micromegas and escape from the planet and because the earth is still in a semimolten state, they head for the planet Mars.

Meanwhile, Thunderbird Smith, having discovered the precise wavelength at which Zoomer's pendant operates, transports himself into microspace. The arrival of his forces triggers an apocalyptic explosion that destroys the newly discovered planet; this marks the creation of our solar system's current planetary alignment. Five billion years later Jack Dagenfort locates Auden Chaplain on an impoverished Mars. Chaplain has kept his identity secret by disguising himself as his wife Leda Chaplain and claiming that Auden himself is dead. Dagenfort is fooled and trapped, and Auden launches into a tirade describing his great accomplishments. He explains that his zero population growth switch works by controlling brain impulses in the hypothalamus. By using radio control, a signal can be sent into an individuals' brain to release or block the hormones necessary for reproduction. He also explains how he worked on Computer Complex and programmed it to use technology to bring humans under control. Auden Chaplain then shows Dagenfort an excavation site in a Martian plain that shows signs of technology in the distant past. Auden believes some sort of advanced technology operated at this site, since local folklore claims that "Gods" once descended from a now absent planet. When Mike Surinat arrives to arrest Auden, the two of them instead piece together the connection between the Glamis-Jules migration to Mars and the beginning of human life on earth; even the pendant, which Auden found on Mars and used to finance his enterprises, becomes part of the connectedness of the worlds in time. The conclusion, reached by means too complicated to spell out here, is that humankind's evolutionary development is deterministic.

Having heard enough of Auden's explanations, Dagenfort asks how Surinat and his entourage were able to reach Mars so quickly. Dagenfort finds to his surprise that it is he who has been transported. While events transpired underground, the red planet was struck by a space time disturbance and a large part of Mars became wedged into the Earth. As the party emerges on the surface, however, Auden has yet another trick to play. He is the inventor of the device linked to universal human brain implants that has enabled Cap-Comm to rule all of humanity. With Cap-Comm gone, Auden activates this device and finds himself in control of the world. He is prevented from retaining this control only by the intervention of a very human, and very ungodlike deus ex machina, Julian Surinat. The latter has been depressed and on various drugs throughout the novel (and was barely visible to the reader) but he now appears and, thanks to having had his brain switch removed during an operation, is able to destroy Auden's control device. Choggles Chaplain, meanwhile, back in the stone age, manages to find a space-time disturbance that leads back to the present. The book ends with her engagement to the narrator Durrant. The final line of the novel reads, "If one legless dreamer can save the world, surely another can win it . . . " (*Hour*, 286).

The dangers of environmental degradation, unmonitored technological advances, genetic tampering, and economic exploitation of both material and human resources are all discussed with passion and imagination in *The Eighty Minute Hour*. However, the debate on the freedom of the will is resolved much more ambiguously. As some of his critics have noted, Aldiss seems to endorse Auden Chaplain's theory of technological evolution, while in the novel humanity only avoids technological determinism through mere chance.[36] Yet Aldiss appears to imply that complete determinism would inhibit survival; he seems to suggest that there is a random factor, an element of chaos, that continually disrupts the apparent order and logic of closed systems. Is this what Julian Surinat's intervention means?

Nevertheless, the power of deterministic processes is felt throughout the book. Perhaps Aldiss is suggesting—and this suggestion would be consistent with ideas of his expressed elsewhere—that there is an eternal struggle between the robotic and the spontaneous and individual in humanity. The dominance of one of these forces only serves to swing a contrary humanity in the opposite direction. While chaos leads to a desperate quest for order, security and progress seem constantly threatened by some primal desire for chaos. If this point is the one Aldiss is making, then we can understand why he wrote *The Eighty Minute Hour* as a comedy, as a demonstration of "hubris clobbered by nemesis" that makes use of the fantastic ideas of science fiction.

In *The Eighty Minute Hour* Aldiss produces a wonderfully styled postmodern fantasy, a metafictional comedy that is not merely a send-up of more conventional science fiction but which stands on its own as an hilarious and sometimes chilling parable of humankind. It is amazing to think that the gifted parodist who wrote *The Saliva Tree* could also fashion this extraordinarily hard-edged, complex, and intellectually probing work.

Brothers of the Head

In 1977, Aldiss published *Brothers of the Head,* a short novel about two rock musicians, Barry and Tom Howe, Siamese twins living at a powerfully evoked place called L'Estrange Head. The twins, we learn, are virtually opposites—Tom is cerebral and introverted, Barry is violent and instinctual—but there slowly grows between them a third head, "the Other," a reconciling principle, as it were, not merely based on the religious idea of "the third eye" but also on Aldiss's notion that science fiction itself is a kind of third eye showing us some of the hidden truths about the world we live in. The twins, whose mother has died in childbirth, are doubly alienated, but things grow worse because they are denied the inner space necessary for reconciliation through "the Other." They suffer the usual fate of rock groups in that they are eventually exploited by commercial management; it is their misfortune to become very popular just because audiences everywhere recognize in them their own divided natures. The story, we realize, can only end in one way. Tom's repression of his animal nature, signaled by the demise of Barry, upsets the natural balance of this unnatural trio and turns the Other into a hostile entity.[37] We cannot achieve the other—the unconscious, the imagination, the balancing perception—without our instinctual selves. If we refuse to recognize hidden possibilities, they may well achieve a shadow dominance over us. And to act out our selfishness, to fail to recognize that we need to embrace a wider reality, to cling to the narrowest definition of what we are, is simply suicidal. (This theme has interesting implications for Aldiss the divided writer, the writer who has been intermittently neglected and overpraised.)

Brothers of the Head was clearly influenced by Olaf Stapledon's omnipresent theme of the divided self and by Walter Miller Jr.'s mutated Rachel—Mrs. Grales from *A Canticle for Leibowitz,* but Aldiss makes the book's rather forced and abstract idea work by keeping the narrative under control and by his ability to produce excellent shorthand takes on contemporary life as both showcase and prison.[38]

Moreau's Other Island

Moreau's Other Island (1980; published in the United States as *An Island Called Moreau,* 1981) is a much more ambitious novel. It continues the Aldiss game of Wells pastiche that began with *The Saliva Tree,* but in this later work Aldiss contrives a viable postcolonial fiction, turning the unacknowledged imperialism and chauvinism of the original Wells novel of 1896 into a parable for the 1980s. In *Moreau's Other Island* Aldiss implicitly condemns the injustices wrought by western science in league with political exploitation of both nature and of the less-developed societies that remain close to nature. At the same time, he relates Wells's Moreau story to the themes of organic life versus mechanism and incorporates into his extension of Wells a lyrical celebration of sexual freedom that the earlier writer would no doubt have approved of, but which is embodied not so much in his work as in that of his contemporary, D. H. Lawrence.

As the story begins, the year is 1996 and a global war is in progress. Calvert Roberts, a U.S. State Department official, is stranded at sea after his space shuttle "Leda" crashes in the Pacific. The opening scene, with Roberts and two of his friends on a raft, quickly establishes the fantastic and speculative mood of this novel and also brings home the parallel with Wells's *The Island of Doctor Moreau,* which also begins with a shipwreck.

No sooner have Roberts and his companions realized their predicament than they notice a dolphin approaching the raft. Is this one of the animals trained by the United States for warfare? Sure enough, a tag showing the Stars and Stripes is seen to be embedded in its tail. Nonetheless, the dolphin, already wounded by the enemy, mistakes the raft for an enemy ship, and the resulting explosion blasts it out of the water, killing both of Roberts' companions.

Through a stroke of luck Roberts survives and eventually drifts to Moreau island, which is marked by a giant letter "M" carved into the cliffs. There he is picked up, as is Wells's hero Prendick, and under similarly disquieting circumstances. The captain of the rescuing boat is Hans Maastricht, who turns out to be foreman of the island enterprise, but the other man, George, is a genetic mutant who is part man, part boar, part hyena. George is member of a race of crossbreeds who were the result of previous experiments upon the island by a man named Moreau. When Roberts struggles to identify the island he is trapped on, he remarks: "Wells also wrote a novel about a Pacific island, nameless as I recall, on which a Dr. Moreau practiced some unpleasant experiments on animals of various kinds. Any connection?"[39] Dart tells him that although Wells may have been writing an allegory, his mythical island really exists.

The Moreau of the piece, as we soon learn, is Mortimer Dart, the master, scientist, and experimenter. Dart is a victim of the thalidomide scandal and was born without legs or arms. This deformity has left him paranoid, vengeful, and resentful toward human society. His own genetic defects impel Dart to discover the potential that drugs may have in a controlled experimental environment. In order to display and maintain superiority over the island's inhabitants, Dart wears a robotic suit with mechanized legs and arms that contain a wide variety of armaments and functions. In his suit Dart is an imposing seven-foot-tall menace, without it he is restricted to his wheelchair and is almost pitifully helpless. In fact, Dart has been brought to Moreau's island by the U.S. government (Roberts was one of the unaware officials who rubberstamped this project) to continue the studies carried out by the original, which Dart considers as crude and primitive but promising enough. He uses the Beast People as a test population for his studies. Dart's assignment is to develop a race of crossbreeds who will prove resistant to the prolonged effects of nuclear radiation. In this age of nuclear war, such a race—known as SRSR's or Stand-by Replacement Sub-Race—will prove essential as a means of productive labor in areas no longer safe for humans.

Once on the spot, Roberts sees the folly of these aims and determines to get the U.S. government to intervene, not suspecting that the operation on the island is a secret American project. He attempts to persuade Dart to radio for American assistance, using his senior government position as leverage. Irritated by Roberts' arrival, Dart refuses to cooperate. After confronting Dart repeatedly, Roberts asks to be let out of the fortified compound where Dart and his several assistants reside. The Beast People in fact live in a small village on the opposite side of the island, and Roberts is told that he will be in danger if he leaves the protection of the compound. As in Wells, the Beast People are not all pleased with the presence of their domineering master and at night they become rebellious and confident.

Maastricht manages to get Roberts to return to the compound and attempts to explain to him that Dart is more than just a power-starved cripple. He explains that unlike Moreau, Dart does not just mutilate and alter the Beast People with his surgery. Dart's creations are genetic mutations—as an example, Maastricht introduces Roberts to a group of seal-like people who have lost their arms and legs while acquiring the ability to breathe underwater.

The friendship developing between Roberts and Maastricht comes to a sudden end when Maastricht is killed in a construction accident. The subsequent funeral scene becomes a pivotal moment within the narrative. Dart, like Moreau, has developed a ritualistic ceremony that he believes is necessary to channel and control the unpredictable and violent emotional power of the Beast People. Dart plays an inspirational hymn and makes a speech in an attempt to place Maastricht's death in a greater context, which might serve to control the Beast People:

> My people, this is a solemn time, when a friend of ours, Hans Maastricht, finally loses his shape. You all know he did wrong and did not obey the Master, which is me. So we bring him here to the death place to be taken up by big Master Underground and in the Sky . . . his whip is bigger than mine, and his wrath is greater, and he's fast, so watch it. It takes a long time to acquire your shape, but not very long to lose it. That's what it's all about. (*Island,* 97)

This speech is followed by a recital of the "creed," which resembles, but is subtly different from, that of Moreau:

> Four Limbs Long
> Wrong Kind of Song
> No cause trouble
>
> Four Limbs Short
> Right Kind of Sport
> No cause trouble
>
> Dare not slay
> Do what he say
> No cause trouble
>
> Speak only speech
> Do what he teach
> No cause trouble
>
> The Master's is the Head that Blames
> The Master's is the Voice that Names
> The Master's is the Hand that Maims
> The Master's is the Whip that Tames
> The Master's is the Wrath that Flames
> (*Island,* 194)

This speech stirs the assembled Beast People to a frenzy, which merely amuses Dart. Roberts, however, notices that several people are missing from the group, including the mutant Foxy, who has been known to cause trouble in the past. Suddenly Foxy bursts onto the scene brandishing Maastricht's riot-gun, which had been assumed to be lost underwater. A group of Beast men respond to Foxy's provocation and chant "Kill! Kill!" The revolution begins. Roberts along with Bernie (half man, half dog) escapes from this mob, although they are separated from Dart.

This episode sets in motion a sequence of encounters that lead to Roberts' awakening from the spiritual and psychological constraints he has lived under as a senior government official. As he flees into the woods, he discovers a small hut that belongs to Jed Warren, a hippie from the sixties. Jed is a navy conscript who has been assigned to work with Dart due to the latter's antisocial tendencies; he does not want to involve himself in Roberts' situation, but from him Roberts learns the true nature of Moreau's island. He realizes that he has long been in denial of the truth, ignoring the horrors that his own government has sponsored and perpetrated. Jed tells him that American nuclear submarines visit the island every month to provide supplies and that Roberts' plan to inform the government and the media of Dart's experiments will simply get him killed. After disclosing these secrets Jed, to protect himself, makes an attempt on Robert's life that fails. Beast People who had been spying on them ambush them, and Jed Warren is eaten alive. Escaping, Roberts jumps off a cliff and lands in the ocean. He believes he has drowned but reawakens in the presence of the Seal People he had met earlier. In his dazed condition he is unsure what they are doing to him but he soon learns; "I gave a great cry as realization dawned on me, and all my limbs trembled in a bout of rapture" (*Island*, 127).

In fact, Roberts has escaped from the nightmare of the island and plunged into an erotic paradise. He is accompanied to Seal Rock, near the main island, by the Seal Woman Lorta and four Seal Men. These Seal People have escaped from civilization and its discontents and are living a life of "oceanic" pleasure, which consists in participation in endless games of love and in pure physicality without jealousy. The presence of the fully formed Japanese child, Satsu, who is only four or five, confirms that Roberts has found a kind of guiltless prenatal paradise, since she too participates to the full in the sexual orgies:

She swam better than her parents, she joined in the love games of the adults. . . For some I paint a picture of depravity. At first, I was shocked by Satsu's love activities, particularly when she was the center of the group's attentions. . . . Their naturalness was such that I quickly became used to everything that went on. (*Island,* 130)

For Roberts this naturalness and sensual release becomes the key to what is missing in the so-called civilized world of restraint and seeming order. The sexuality of the Seal People contrasts sharply with the "play girl" antics of Dart's attractive assistant, Heather. She is a product of self-conscious liberation; they are simply natural, and whereas Roberts distrusts his own impulses in relation to Heather, he is liberated by his connection with the Seal People. (Appropriately, they call him "Calvary," even while they are freeing him from his cross of conflict and repression.) At the same time, by giving them the gift of fire he almost becomes their Promethean transformer; at the end he wonders whether he has not destroyed them by doing so. Whatever the result for them (and the text suggests that he will help them survive), the result for Roberts is positive. After his encounter with the Seal People, he is psychologically transformed and determines to free the Beast People from Dart's and his own government's bondage. Returning to the island, Roberts finds the "good" mutant George impaled on a pole, rather like one of Kurtz's victims in Conrad's *Heart of Darkness.* Roberts reaches the radio room, where he is able to signal his department to send a rescue helicopter. Shortly after, Dart imprisons him in a small cage on the edge of the compound's laboratory. Bernie releases him, warning that Foxy is about to set fire to the compound. By this time Roberts understands Foxy's need for violent protest.

Roberts helps set Dart's headquarters on fire, and the climax occurs as the supply submarine arrives and the navy and the Beast People attack each other. Equipped in his robotic weapons suit, Dart is ready to rally the navy troops, but Foxy appears on a rooftop and shoots him. Dart's body is carried aboard the submarine. Roberts, accompanied by the Seal People, awaits the arrival of his rescue helicopter.

Much of this novel uses approaches and discourses reminiscent of colonial and postcolonial writing.[40] The themes of freedom and liberation loom large, and the use of pseudoprimitive dialects is carried beyond Wells's mock rituals. *Moreau's Other Island* is framed by an opening segment entitled "To Sink Below" and an ending segment "The

Light Died," each written in third-person narration and printed in italicized type. These sections, which form a lyrical prelude and postlude to the novel, speak of the ocean and its life force and suggest the ultimate frame of reference of Aldiss's book. The separate but contiguous worlds of land and water are analogous to the conscious and unconscious mind of humankind:

> The conscious brain is accustomed to a regular series of waking and sleeping states which correspond to light and dark. Matters are less clearcut in the unconscious: a different set of clocks ticks. The unconscious has its own submarine element, unpunctuated by sun. The difference is between Reason, which invented the twenty-four hour clock, and instinct, which keeps its own Great Time. Until humanity comes to an armistice between these yin-yang factors there is no armistice possible on Earth. The bombs will fall. (*Island*, 174)

Unlike William Golding, whose *Lord of the Flies* has a similar setting and themes, Aldiss does not evoke Christian notions of original sin to extend and complexify the Darwinian realm Wells wrestled with and despaired of transcending. Aldiss opts instead for a post-Lawrencian sexuality and a post-Jungian vision of the reintegration of consciousness and the unconscious. The influence of the sixties, Eastern thought, and perspectives derived from Conrad, Freud, and Levi-Strauss enable him to transform the original Moreau story into a parable for our time, taking us beyond crude Darwinism to ecology and beyond conditioned guilt to a naturalness that suggests the possibility of spiritual rebirth and reintegration with nature.[41] Given its ingenuity of structure, its richness of reference, its relevance to the central issues of our time—political, ecological, and psychological—*Moreau's Other Island* must be considered one of Brian Aldiss's best science fiction novels.

Dracula Unbound

In 1991 Aldiss returned to the intertextual game with a full-length novel based on another of the great myths of western society. *Dracula Unbound* is a half-serious but mostly jocular takeoff on the famous story, written in a style quite adequate to the limited aims of the text. Resurrecting Bram Stoker's eternally compelling hero in the familiar territory of his own house and Oxford environs, Aldiss produces a fast-paced narrative that sometimes seems to trip over itself, especially at the conclusion. But despite the book's glossy competence, the enterprise itself becomes rather suspect in view of its almost too-perfect timing, following as it did the release of the Roger Corman *Frankenstein Unbound* and expertly coordinated as it was with the revival of the Dracula theme in the media everywhere.

In short, *Dracula Unbound* is the kind of book that writers' agents applaud, an opportunistic book but one that forms no significant part of the Aldiss oeuvre. And—as often happens in such cases—the calculations failed to add up to either a literary triumph or to a new film. Another way of looking at it is to say that by the early 1990s, the significant Brian Aldiss fictions had to be sought in his mainstream contemporary novels, specifically in the concluding books of what he had decided to call the Squire Quartet. Aldiss had at last turned his creative energy away from mainstream science fiction as well as from literary games, those variations on fantastic themes that had tempted him for so long. By the early 1990s he had achieved the ambition manifested in his untidy but challenging new wave fiction of the 1960s: leaving aside a few minor literary forays, Brian Aldiss had written himself out of science fiction.

Chapter Five
The Mainstream Fiction

The Big Bow-Wow strain I can do myself like any now going; but the exquisite touch, which renders ordinary commonplace things and characters interesting, from the truth of the description and the sentiment, is denied to me.

—Sir Walter Scott (praising Jane Austen), *Journal* (1826)

Brian Aldiss, unlike of most of his science fiction writing contemporaries, has attempted to "do" both worlds referred to in Sir Walter Scott's well-known comparison between his work and the novels of Jane Austen. Not content with the "Big Bow-Wow strain" of his epic science fiction, Aldiss has moved gradually in the direction of rendering the "commonplace things" that mostly intrigue the mainstream novelist. This shift in focus is less surprising when we remember that Aldiss began as a mainstream writer, one with a strong gift for transforming familiar everyday existence into quietly memorable fiction. From the beginning—even while he was busy planning and writing other stories that approach the wildest fantasy—he succeeded in capturing what Randall Jarrell has called "the dailyness of life," the commonplace touched with a miraculous sense of truth.[1]

The Brightfount Diaries

Brian Aldiss's first published novel, *The Brightfount Diaries,* for example, is the fictional record of Peter, a young (and rather naive) 25-year-old assistant in Brightfount's Bookstore, an old-fashioned establishment located in an imaginary but quite typical English university town of the 1950s.[2] Peter's diary is a chronicle of the everyday goings-on in the small circle of Brightfount's Bookstore and its (surprisingly numerous) employees and among Peter's neighbors and relatives. Notable among the second group are Uncle Leo and Aunt Anne (the latter at first beguiles the young man with her ingenious but quite false recollections of Uncle Leo's encounters with D. H. Lawrence), as well as Peter's landlady Vera Yell, his cousin Derek and Derek's wife Myra—the latter couple being a trifle more worldly wise, and spoiled, than the young hero. Aldiss's first novel is remarkable for the speed of its narrative and its consistently sharp but low-key observation, not to mention the sheer sense of human goodness and simplicity that the writer evokes, without the slightest trace of sentimentality or self-consciousness. In writing it Aldiss drew upon his postwar experience in an Oxford bookshop, suppressing all his bitter army memories; it appealed to a strife-weary public and parts were printed in *The Bookseller,* a trade magazine.[3] Faber & Faber soon made an offer to publish, but the book's distance from the real mood of England in the 1950s may be measured by comparing it with D. B. Wyndham Lewis's acerbic London novel of 1951, *Rotting Hill.*[4]

Nonetheless, although *The Brightfount Diaries* is idyllic, it is stylistically consistent and acute to a degree. Those who, like the present writer, experienced the English life of this period in such a setting will testify to the novel's truth of representation, but almost any reader will warm to its unforced humor, which creates the effect of a genre painting; in short, it is a skilled evocation but one that trades depth and dramatic contrast for a very gentle shock of recognition.

The diary runs from June to December and ends with a Christmas party at the bookstore. Aldiss's narrator and innocent hero is extraordinarily well-rendered; he is kind, rather passive, and baffled by everything. In his small unviolent, almost cozy world, he is rather incompetent but never ridiculous, never outrightly the fool. Though it may ultimately evoke a world that never was, except in the imagination of English writers, painters, and musicians—many of whom created similar "pastoral" corners populated by gently observed and accurately rendered ordinary people—*The Brightfount Diaries* is a completely satisfying fiction. The bookstore and its circle remain untroubled by historical distractions, such as war, poverty, or nuclear threat. In such a world, Darwin, Dostoevski, and Freud do not exist. Many comic works draw their point from the disparity between a character's desires or self-image and his or her "real-life" situation. But very few of the inhabitants of the Brightfount world suffer from a fundamental illusion about who they are or what they can aspire to. The people in Aldiss's novel seem content; they spend most of their time doing small things with a certain relish, including being funny in a harmless way. While Aldiss indulges in frequent in-jokes about writing and publishing and delivers a number of ingenious literary puns, the real comedy in the Brightfount world derives from the wonderful way in which the writer catalogs the small incompetencies and minor follies of human nature. It is this effortless rendering of the foibles of the hero, his relatives, the bookstore staff, the customers, and the "travelers," or publisher's representatives that carries the reader along and gives delight.

All of these qualities, perhaps surprisingly, seem to have very little connection with the work of Kingsley Amis and the Angry Young Men, the postwar British school of fiction writers who delighted in breaking traditional taboos in the name of a new working class ethic and aesthetic. Aldiss's novel rather points us back to such works as Arnold Bennett's *Riceyman Steps,* to George Grossmith's *Diary of a Nobody,* back to H. G. Wells's *Kipps,* to the rather inefficient, unthreatening world of the small English shopkeeper. The book is almost plotless, and while it lacks the broad comedy of Wells and Grossmith or the pathos of Bennett's *Riceyman Steps,* it is all the more compelling and credible for that. And although he might not welcome the comparison, Aldiss's book, because it offers us an intriguing glimpse of a circumscribed and essentially Edenic world, belongs also in the same category as James Herriot's *All Things Great and Small.* Dressed up in a suitable production, the subject matter would appeal to the same kind of mass audience as the television version of Herriot's work, especially as we draw further away from—and so become more nostalgic about—the individualism and eccentricity that were an integral part of such vanished communities and self-sufficient enterprises.

The Male Response

After launching his career as a science fiction writer with *Non-Stop* and other works, Brian Aldiss returned to mainstream fiction in 1961 with *The Male Response: A Timely Original Story.* The book is much wittier than its title implies and remains readable, although its indebtedness to both Evelyn Waugh and Aldous Huxley is so blatant as to be disconcerting.[5] The British protagonist Soames Noyes, a computer salesman ahead of his time, visits the new state of Goya in Africa. He soon goes native, crossing paths with a witch doctor and getting hopelessly entangled with various beautiful women. After participating in an outrageous public sexual rite, Noyes becomes king of Goya, only to be tricked by the witch doctor into kicking a venomous snake, which quickly disposes of our hero. Noyes's idiotic insouciance is wonderfully conveyed by Aldiss, but the book's mood, the character of Noyes, the setting and style of humor are all derived from Huxley and Waugh. Aldiss's approach to things African has also dated badly, since this tale of Englishman-foiled-by-odd-but-deadly-tribesmen is distinctly colonial, despite its satire, and has more in common with the perspectives of Joyce Cary's *Mister Johnson* and Evelyn Waugh's *Black Mischief* than with Amos Tutuola or Chinua Achebe.

The Horatio Stubbs Trilogy

In the early 1970s Brian Aldiss returned to mainstream fiction, this time to deal with a subject matter very far removed from the everyday life of small shopkeepers but one that continued the Waugh connection, although in quite another fashion. The Horatio Stubbs trilogy clearly derives from the more personal and pungent aspects of Aldiss's war experience and is written in a very different style and tone from anything he had done previously. While the writer himself saw this as liberating, the reader coming to these books some decades later might very well take another view.

The trilogy begins with *The Hand-Reared Boy* (1970) and includes *A Soldier Erect* (1971) and *A Rude Awakening* (1978). It was apparently intended to be Aldiss's "war work," an unbuttoned and very ungenteel version of Evelyn Waugh's *Sword of Honour* books.[6] Like Waugh, Aldiss focuses on those aspects of World War II experience that carry us close to absurdity, and both writers establish their protagonists as centers of integrity amid the general dishonesty, incompetence, and violence of the world in which they move.

There, however, the resemblance ends, for while Waugh manages to create an impressive panorama of social change and to convey, in prose as sharp as a stiletto, a near-tragic sense of loss amid the foolishness of war, Aldiss uses his trilogy, especially the first two books, to project sexual fantasies, which, although bold and even amusing to begin with, soon begin to pall on the reader.[7]

The Horatio Stubbs trilogy for much of its length reads like a very calculated and self-conscious piece of erotica, that is to say the narrative excludes almost everything that does not have to do with the sexual experience of the young hero. The books are not, however, a very ingenious or creative venture into erotica, which is how one might describe the work of Anais Nin, who—it could be argued—turns this genre into subtle art. Whereas Anais Nin details the many-layered psychological reverberations of almost every kind of sexuality and transcends gender-fixations, the Horatio Stubbs trilogy with its baldly graphic and phallic-centered sexuality resembles the one-dimensional underground male erotica of the eighteenth century and Victorian eras.[8]

The first book in the series, *The Hand-Reared Boy*, with its cheap punning title, sets the tone. It describes the young life of the hero almost exclusively in terms of his obsession with masturbation and introduces other characters and events only in relation to the diversity of situations in which this particular form of sexuality can be practiced. Horatio's brother, sister, and schoolmates appear as partners in this activity, which is never really described in experiential terms but is cataloged in all its variations as to time, place, and partner. The novel in fact presents little or no psychological complexity; pleasure is noted but no particular guilt is registered, and the ramifications in Horatio's emotional life are not explored. Nor, though the masturbation is practiced mostly by males, is there more than casual acknowledgment of the homoerotic side; the masturbating is seen merely as a kind of substitute for the mature heterosexual congress that the protagonist aspires to and eventually achieves.

In *The Hand-Reared Boy*, Aldiss's descriptions of the sexual experience, although restrained, are oversimplified and ultimately monotonous: he must therefore find another means of enlisting the reader's attention. He attempts to do this by introducing a love affair between Horatio and one of his female teachers, surrounding the woman with a mystery and ambiguity that the novel unfortunately fails to develop in depth or to resolve.

The Hand-Reared Boy opens with a high tea given by Horatio's (rather naive) mother for her 17-year-old son's teacher, Virginia Traven. As Horatio blatantly informs us in the course of this event (the narrative is in the first person), he has had sex with everyone in the room, only excepting his mother, and is in the miseries/splendors of calf-love for Virginia. The narrative then goes back to fill in Horatio's life, almost from birth, although only in the very narrow dimensions already indicated. At the end we return to the relationship between Horatio and Virginia, which carries on (although not sexually) when the young man leaves home and moves to London. Horatio finds that far from being her only lover, he has for a rival one of the young men of his school, who was first in her bed and still pursues her jealously. Despite the efforts of the two young men to unravel the mystery of Virginia (Who and what does she love? Is she innocent or vicious? A liar or a hurt woman? Is she complex or just elusive?), the book ends with neither the young protagonist nor the reader any the wiser. Britain, meanwhile, stands poised on the verge of the Second World War and Horatio is about to enter the service and change his life, but not his obsession with sex, forever.

A Soldier Erect, with its explanatory subtitle: "Being the further adventures of the Hand-Reared Boy," appeared only a year after its predecessor, which had sold very well and achieved a minor *success de scandale* with the British public.[9] The title pun is once again disconcertingly obvious, and this novel is, if anything, less successful than the first. The blatant and unredeemed brutality of some of its pages, the obviousness of the style and manner, seems to be the result of miscalculation, since Aldiss has often shown himself to be a writer capable of transmuting the most unlikely materials.

In this novel Stubbs finds himself in India and Burma. The Japanese forces are still formidable and the British "forgotten army" is slowly organized to resist them. The chaotic conditions of war, rendered directly and sometimes brutally although not particularly memorably, are heavily foregrounded by Stubbs' relentless search for the next available prostitute. The dishonesty and the physical filth of army existence are everywhere strongly emphasized, but the text does not put these into sharp perspective, while Aldiss's attempts at comedy often come off as merely grotesque. Something is clearly wrong with this narrative, and a comparison with the Waugh trilogy helps us to understand that *A Soldier Erect* suffers from a certain imaginative constriction. Whereas Waugh in his rendering of the military casts documentation aside and constructs ingenious absurdities in a Chinese box superimposition on "the way it was," Aldiss refuses to let go of fact and memory and tries to derive his comedy from a perseverating reality—not a good prescription for artistic complexity. The following passages from *A Rude Awakening* reveal quite clearly the undigested nature of the emotional material presented; they mark the two anchoring emotional poles of the book: erotic hunger and war, and it will be clear that in neither case is the issue clarified for the reader.

> Her arms were rather spotty, but we were getting on quite well when I noticed Nelson preparing to slip out with Valerie. He winked at me, a slow thorough wink that must have bruised his eyeball. Dirty bastard! Jealousy seized me. Valerie wasn't bad. A bit hefty owing to her involvement in the Woman's Land Army, but very cheerful—and everyone understood that Land Army girls needed it regular; the contact with agriculture made them that way. They would be going to the pub for a pint and afterwards Nelson would get her against our back wall for a knee-trembler.[10]

The whole site was mud, gouged by shells and trenches and running boots; bits of men, whole limbs, had been blasted all about the area. The dead bodies, fat and blackened in the heat, had at last been dragged away; but the bits that had fallen off or been blown off or shot off or chopped off, still lay about, and poisoned the air with the stomach-curdling sweet stench of carrion. (*Awakening,* 246)

Both passages represent raw experience untransformed by art and as such they are merely unpleasant rather than funny or powerful. Here, the writer's overanxious desire to shock makes claims on the reader that are best described as vulgar, that is, too blatant in their attention-seeking obviousness. If one compares the first passage to almost any similar scene in the work of Aldiss's contemporaries, Kingsley Amis and John Braine—and there are many such passages—its crudeness becomes apparent. Grim, after-the-battle scenes in Hemingway, Mailer, or even in popular films such as *Patton,* reveal the Aldiss rendering of the battlefield as a mere catalog.

A Rude Awakening, the third volume of the Stubbs trilogy, does not really escape the problems of the other books, although postwar Suma-tra, an unusual setting, is well-rendered, and the hero's eternal itch is comically but quite trenchantly set in historical context. Here Horatio Stubbs' sexual adventures are played out in a decadent multiracial soci-ety; Aldiss has come a long way in political sophistication—although not in artistic subtlety—from *The Male Response.* His sense of the quick-ness of the obsolescence of British power in the post-World War II world, especially in Asia, anticipates an important part of *Forgotten Life,* but the banalities that mar the earlier volumes in this series are res-olutely sustained:

"The bloody Chinese . . ." I thought. "Mid-afternoon! . . ." They were at it all the time. What else was there to do when you were stuck in a coun-try paralysed by revolution, preceded by three years of servitude under the scum of the earth? As banks closed, everywhere thighs were bound to open, the lips of those neat little eastern twots to unfurl like buds, and fornication to commence. The savory sounds from next door illustrated my thesis; I clutched my prick and wondered at the laws of the globe. (*Awakening,* 70)

It would be hard to construct a paragraph that combines cliché, superficial epithet, and overall cheapness of effect in such brief compass, yet this novel contains many of equal banality.

A Rude Awakening failed to sell as well as the first two volumes of the trilogy. The tediousness of many of its pages is enough to account for that, but perhaps the public was simply growing tired of listening to a narrator who never seems able to rise above the crudest language or perceptions of reality.

The Squire Quartet

Life in the West, which appeared in 1980, proved a welcome change from such self-indulgent fiction.[11] It is an intelligent and well-structured mainstream novel—few better have been written by writers so strongly identified throughout their careers with genre fiction. Aldiss was to go on to write three related and equally excellent novels during the 1980s and 1990s, completing the so-called Squire Quartet in 1994 with *Somewhere East of Life.*

Aldiss's protagonist, Tom Squire, who gives his name to the series, plays an important role only in this first novel. In fact, one of the problems for the reader seeking to come to terms with the quartet as a whole is that each novel introduces different central characters and ends without fully resolving the issues focused in that character. Unlike Lawrence Durrell's *Alexandria Quartet,* Aldiss's novels do not attempt to explore a complex reality from many perspectives but rather move through our era from the latter stages of the cold war to an imagined near-future, showing the impact of social and political changes on the lives of upper-middle-class Britishers of the professional and intellectual castes.

Tom Squire, the central figure of *Life in the West,* is neither an academic nor a professional writer but an even more representative late-twentieth-century intellectual, in that his ideas and his influence are conveyed through the mass media and in conversations at specialist conferences. As a learned television host who takes on the role of analyst and innovative presenter of ideas and trends in visual form, Squire is a phenomenon of our post-McLuhan age. Sir Kenneth Clark and Alistair Cooke were early real-life embodiments of this type, but many have followed: James Burke, Michael Wood, and Sister Wendy in England; Carl Sagan and others in North America.

Aldiss, however, set his imagination to work on this kind of television *cicerone* some time before the species became common. He uses Squire to underline the point that mass media are the premier cultural instigators of our time, since most ideas reach ordinary people through them. Aldiss never dismisses mass culture, however, even when he satirizes the

academic penchant to inflate its importance or when he has fun with the
absurd gap between academic analysis and the trivial artifacts it pro-
nounces upon. Squire's status as TV guru enables Aldiss to show how in
our time private life—not to mention political and artistic expression—
are controlled and dominated by the media.

Life in the West appeared at a time when the cold war was still a nag-
ging fact, and strong barriers existed to the free flow of information
between east and west. Since 1980, life in both the former communist
countries and the west has been increasingly shaped by American popular culture. Aldiss means us to see Tom Squire's affair with the television
"sex symbol" Laura Nye not only as a personal act on the part of his protagonist but also as a symbol of a certain kind of obsession, one that
increasingly plagues the world in general.

Tom Squire is not merely a media figure, however: he is also a member of the traditional privileged gentry class, the squire of Pippet Hall, a
house Aldiss locates in his native Norfolk. Here, tradition and family
values count for much. Even though he is physically and imaginatively
involved with the beautiful Laura, Squire decides in the end to give her
up and return to his wife, who barely tolerates him, so as not to sacrifice
the tradition at Pippet Hall. However appealing Laura is as sexual partner and coworker, she simply would not do as the mistress of the family
estate. (Or so he seems to decide; in the fourth Squire novel, however,
we see that Laura does acquire a country house and a genteel husband.)

Squire's midlife crisis is resolved by the reestablishment of his connections with his family and the past, and this resolution is not seen by
Aldiss as merely a retreat on his part or a failure. So far as his marital
infidelities are concerned, Squire assuages his guilt by some intellectual
acrobatics: he decides that biology makes it impossible for most men to
remain faithful to their wives; women on the other hand, have good reason to stick to the nest. This rationalization allows him to indulge in a
near murderous rage when his wife Teresa takes a lover, while brushing
off his own indulgences as mere peccadilloes. In the face of his provoca-
tions, Teresa adopts the familiar "Hera" stance, railing at her erring
Zeus, becoming a shrew and a carping critic at the hearthside, and
finally abandoning him when he seems to need her most. Teresa tells
Squire that "all I need is your silence," which this public communicator
rightly takes as a crushing rebuke.

Not only does Squire fall out with his wife, he almost wrecks the
Ermalpa conference on future culture with his intransigence and bitterness, which take the form of strong anti-Marxist outbursts directed at a

few of the delegates and at his close working associate Jacques d'Exiteuil. It soon becomes apparent that the break with d'Exiteuil is permanent, and the latter predicts that Squire is finished as an academic force, since Marxism is bound to remain a central ideology among scholars, a prediction—if Aldiss indeed believed it—that, despite the fall of the Soviet system, seems to have been fulfilled. The irony is that it is his relationship with the actual representative of the Soviet system, Professor Rugorsky, that brings out Squire's guilt—and his charity. While he refuses to chastise himself for his treatment of Teresa, he is bitterly upset when he later decides that he has let Rugorsky down, allowing him to return to Moscow to face charges of corruption that may result in the death penalty.

Even so, Aldiss is not very hard on his protagonist's failings. Squire is seen always as a decent enough fellow; he does not attempt to manipulate situations to achieve power; he is not a poseur, nor is he, despite his outbursts, a terribly self-indulgent man. He is in fact something of an innocent, with that touch of that half-malicious sycophancy that goes along with a desire for peace at almost any cost. To be sure, Squire loses control in the face of ideological Marxism and inevitably sounds like a bitter old Tory, which his associates (who do not know him deeply) immediately relate to his actual status in British society. As Aldiss makes abundantly clear, however, Squire really does believe in humanity, rather than any ideology. In the end we see him as a rather sad and thoroughly disillusioned liberal agnostic, one who can achieve faith in neither God nor in the future, but who has nonetheless found a kind of center, however tenuous, in himself and in his personal relation to tradition. Squire is about as close as we could expect to get in the 1970s to Ford Madox Ford's Christopher Tietjens, the ultimately decent but misunderstood fogy, although Tietjens was a self-declared Tory, as was Ford, while Squire denies being one, at least as a voter.[12] Despite the traditional form, however, Aldiss pens no elegy for Tory values: while Squire might consent to hobnob with Evelyn Waugh's Guy Crouchback and might empathize with his painful adjustments to our century, he would certainly regard him as a fossil. Aldiss's sense of his own time is exemplary.

Hardly dazzling in style, but effective and steady, *Life in the West* shows Aldiss coming close to writers like J. B. Priestley, C. P. Snow, the later Anthony Burgess, or Kingsley Amis—in short, this is good reliable middle-brow fiction.

Life in the West, in fact, seems to have left science fiction far behind— a situation neatly summed up in Squire's reflection in chapter 10 that science fiction cannot reflect the complexities of the world of 1970—as witness the happenings at the conference. Squire's unexpected sighting of a UFO at Ermalpa and his dismissal of the phenomenon seem to confirm Aldiss's subtext: that he must distance himself from these familiar literary games, from his favored science fiction genre, in order to achieve a deeper fictional truth. Despite this subtext, some ideas of Olaf Stapledon, the great British speculative writer of the thirties, infiltrate Aldiss's vision. The Stapledonian perspective (even though Stapledon was once a communist) suggests that ordinary humans have to deal with what nature, biology, and society deal out to them and that this cannot be changed in any full sense by utopian or revolutionary action: the latter merely shuffles the deck, so to speak, creating as many problems as it solves. What is lacking in Aldiss's mainstream version of this perspective is any ultimate leap of faith: no sense of the power of mind to change old affiliations or to transcend social impasse. Squire is denied even the bleak consolation of Stapledon's Star Maker.

In the end, Thomas Squire, like Professor Godfrey St. Peter in Willa Cather's *The Professor's House* (another humanist intellectual at a life crisis), decides that he must learn to live without joy. We see him facing the necessity of life with Teresa, stripped of illusions, motivated to carry on by his half-skeptical allegiance to a flawed but "decent" tradition.

Forgotten Life, the second book of the Squire Quartet, published in 1988, introduces a strong counterforce to this tolerated gentility. The book captures important aspects of the English experience during World War II and the postwar decades, and in it Aldiss seems to redraft the material of the Stubbs trilogy from a much deeper perspective. *Forgotten Life* also represents a largely successful attempt by Aldiss to create fiction out of what is clearly obsessive childhood material.[13]

In this novel, attempting to achieve maximum depth and resonance in his main character, Aldiss adopts the technique of doubling. The foreground is occupied by Clement Winter, an Oxford don, a reserved, cautious, and introverted man, married to a restless, anxious woman, Sheila Tomlinson, who also happens to be a very successful fantasy writer. Much of the book deals with their relationship; even more central, however, is Clement Winter's relationship with his dead brother, Joseph, whose letters and memoirs he is in the process of editing. The Joseph Winter material enables Aldiss to create a kind of powerful shadow figure for Clement, for, although Joseph is an intellectual and writer, there is nothing donnish about him. His war experiences, his sexual adventures, his leftist views and social activism, mostly recorded in the documents examined by Clement, force the latter to reexamine his own life, which is approaching a point of crisis.

The book opens as Sheila is returning from a very successful North American tour, one designed to promote her "Green Mouth" novels, a fantasy series focusing on the imaginary planet of Kerinth.[14] Clement Winter is a Jungian analyst, as well as a professor, and Sheila, we learn, had been one of his early patients. Contrary to the information conveyed on the dust jackets of her books, Sheila's childhood was a miserable one (she was raped by a drunken stepfather). Her talisman during that bleak time was a toy alligator named Green Mouth, which has since become the marketing and cult symbol of her fantasy books. She herself is known as Green Mouth, wears appropriate green lipstick and otherwise indulges herself (and her fans) with grotesque, but profitable, charades. Unfortunately for Clement, she has also recently indulged herself in a blatant affair with one of her New York editors, and she eventually leaves her husband to be with this lover. Only in the last sentence of the story, when Clement hears her key in the lock of their Oxford house, are we given some sense that the marital ties created between the two might be strong enough to overcome her passion. Since the Winters' faithful French live-in housekeeper has also recently decamped to join a lover, Clement has the experience of being twice bereft, both times as a result of a kind of passionate commitment that seems very alien to his own methodical, unromantic, and dutiful way of being.

While these events are developing, Clement has become the voyeur of his dead brother's life experience. These memories include some striking reminiscences of the Second World War, obviously based on Aldiss's own time in service. Clement is well aware that his brother had always considered his own childhood to be one of misery, due to what he perceived as their mother's blatant indifference to him. Joseph believed until the end of his life not only that his mother had emotionally abandoned him but that she never loved him, having given all of her affection to their sister Ellen. Equally hurtful, his parents placed him in the worst kind of English schools, places that fostered his bitterness and turned his life into a running battle with middle-class life and privilege. Aldiss records Joseph's anger with some ferocity, suggesting that this issue runs deep for him, as does the question of perceived parental indifference:

> Cuisine of course is not the strong point of schools. One goes there to learn, not to eat. Eating is incidental. It is Learning that maketh Gentle-

men. All it could possibly make at St. Paul's, to put things at their unlikely best, was to turn out snotty little trumped-up sons of small tradesmen. Only Gentlemen make Gentlemen. It's a closed shop. You need inherited money, lawns down to lakes, Paters in Who's Who, horses in the paddock, friendships with judges, and a fucking blase accent to be a Gentlemen. You need to steer clear of St. Paul's, where a notice in the sports field made it plain that it was a Preparatory School, without clarifying what exactly it might be preparing you for. Not Eton or Harrow, that's for sure.[15]

During the course of examining his brother's papers, Clement has an uncanny experience: he believes he sees Joseph's ghost. The figure speaks to him and tells him that "everything came out all right." This statement is confirmed by other documents and by Lucy, Joseph's last lover. The documents report a recurring dream of arrival at a magical gate; they also record an actual trip to an ordinary English seashore hotel with Lucy, one that seems to put the final seal on Joseph's transformation. At the hotel, according to Joseph's account and Lucy's testimony, Joseph bathes his naked body in radiant moonlight and invokes the muse with passionate sincerity. Later that night he has a dream in which an oracular female figure reassures him that his mother did in fact love him. Although Clement is not given to such extravagant experiences, in his capacity as a Jungian analyst, he must accept his brother's transformation as meaningful and genuine.

The title *Forgotten Life* thus refers not only to Joseph but equally to Clement. Joseph has recovered his lost past and healed himself of a troubling psychic wound. Clement, on the other hand, seems to have forgotten how to live. A good man, who has real love and much tolerance for both his wife and his brother, he seems utterly ineffective as a human being. His story ends inconclusively, and in a very unsatisfactory manner. In this respect, we can see some miscalculation on the part of Aldiss the novelist. For one thing, while Clement's donnish nature is skillfully evoked, we never quite believe in him as an analyst. It seems clear, in fact, that Aldiss has made him a Jungian simply in order to make the connection with Joseph's symbolic and transformative experiences. Jungians, like Freudians, Marxists, feminists, and ecologists, see much of reality through their ideological spectacles. Clement's waking life gives little evidence of any Jungian perceptions; he hardly has a single "Jungian" thought in the course of the book. (He does not even interpret his ghostly vision of Joseph in a Jungian manner!) It is like creating a novel about an athlete who never once thinks of sport. This fact points to a weakness of structure in the novel. Of course it would have been possible to create a fiction encompassing the contrasting lives of two brothers, one who makes sense of his life and who fails to do so. Aldiss's ending, however, does not suggest that such was his intention; he simply seems unable to find a way to bring Clement's experiences to a satisfactory resolution. *Forgotten Life* is in many respects a successful fiction, but the incompleteness of Aldiss's presentation of his main character prevents the novel from being a truly satisfying experience for the reader.

The book, however, was generally well received both by critics and by the public, as it deserved to be.[16] What is curious is that when Aldiss decided to write sequels to *Life in the West* and *Forgotten Life,* he failed to develop the main characters of either novel, but instead used them in subsidiary roles in the last two volumes of the so-called Squire Quartet. Unfortunately, this tends to reduce these characters to caricatures, when what the reader might have expected was a deepening of understanding of interesting figures like Tom Squire and Clement Winter.

In 1993 Aldiss published *Remembrance Day,* dedicated to Doris Lessing, a novel structured around a sociological inquiry, but one that the novelist uses to mask an existential probe, much in the manner of Thornton Wilder's *The Bridge of San Luis Rey.* In the first brief chapter we are at an academic conference in Florida. A visiting British professor, Gordon Levine, meets a colorful American academic, Hengist Morton Embry, an ambitious theorist of "stochastic sociology." Embry is planning a year's sabbatical leave in Norfolk, where he intends to investigate the circumstances surrounding a 1986 hotel explosion at Great Yarmouth, one connected with IRA terrorism; four people were killed.

> "Who were the four persons killed that day? What were their lives like?" Embry asks. "What brought them to that hotel on that date? Was their presence merely stochastic, or had it to do with, say, economic conditions?"
>
> "Or the hand of God," hinted Levine, smiling.
>
> "We are open-minded. We rule nothing out. Not even the Immanent Will. *'Veni redemptor.'* I do not go into this project with preconceived ideas, Gordy. I want to establish whether the random was at work, or were those deaths circumstance-chain deaths—with submerged social causation of the same kind that draws me back to ancestral ground?"[17]

The next four parts of the novel lead us deeply into the lives of the victims of the explosion: the first of these sections takes place in Norfolk in the summer of 1986; the second describes events in Prague in the spring of the same year; the third goes back to 1981 to chronicle a marital breakup among the 1980s nouveau riche; the fourth carries on the Norfolk narrative and propels some of the characters toward the fatal encounter. The last section returns us to Professor Embry's 1991 investigation and discloses his findings.

The first, or Norfolk summer episode, is relaxed, almost casual in its focus on Ray and Ruby Tebbut, a good-natured but hedged-in middle-aged couple whose fortunes have declined with the economy. They are living with Ruby's ancient mother, Agnes Silcock, in a ramshackle Norfolk country cottage, both working to keep things going and enjoying the simple pleasures of pub, afternoon tea, and an occasional tumble in bed. Tebbut, half-unwillingly, but in his slack, good-natured way, assumes a 300 pound debt to help an ungrateful casual acquaintance, Michael Linwood, the son of a well-off eccentric father, who keeps him poor. Linwood and his family dodge the debt, although they realize it will strain the Tebbuts' budget. It strains not only the budget but the Tebbuts' relationship; just when things are getting explosive, the Tebbuts' daughter Jennifer comes to visit, bringing a mysterious Czech male friend named Jaroslav Vacek. The chapter ends with the daughter and her friend heading to Yarmouth.

In the next section we learn that Vacek is an opportunistic and cynical Czech communist. He enlists a rather feckless and down-at-heel filmmaker named Petrik to go on an errand to Germany for him. Petrik's girlfriend, who travels with him, has already casually slept with the Irishman, an IRA contact, whom they are assigned to watch on the train. The Irishman knocks out Petrik and steals a parcel of money he was supposed to be carrying to Germany for Vacek. Vacek, we learn, is soon to go to London.

In chapter 4 we meet Dominick and Fenella Mayor, who are part of Britain's post-Thatcher computer millionaire set. Their opulent but somewhat pretentious and vulgar surroundings and lifestyle are brilliantly evoked by Aldiss, who stops short of satire to convey the breakdown of their marriage with chilling power. We empathize strongly with both the harried Dominick (it turns out he is a Russian-born orphan) and the half-mad and willful Fenella. One marvelous comic scene follows another; Aldiss is here at his peak, doing top-drawer Waugh for the 1980s. When Fenella retreats to her dead mother's house in Scotland, Dominick (despite some helpful consultations with Clement Winter) retires in disarray, eventually to remarry and father two more children. At this point he buys the Dionoya Hotel in Norfolk, where, a few years later, an Irish guest who calls himself Jim Donnell takes up residence.

Chapter 5 takes us back to midsummer 1986 and the Tebbuts. Walking in the country, Ruby has a vision of an old woman who tells her, "People saw you die by the seaside." (Her old mother had just complained about never being taken there.) This somber moment is nearly forgotten as old Mr. Linwood invites the Tebbuts to dinner with the local gentry, Sir Thomas and Lady Teresa Squire. The dinner is another of the novel's comic triumphs; smooth conversation and British manners conceal the differences among the guests, but the evening ends with an outburst of melodrama. The next day, however, old Linwood pays Ray his 300 pounds and the Tebbuts (who have also received money from Ruby's sister) decide to join their daughter for a holiday at "a comfortable little hotel" in Yarmouth.

The final section of the novel, entitled "Salvation," returns to Professor Hengist Morton Embry. He presents his findings on the 1986 explosion to Gordon Levine and Sir Alistair Stern, the principal of "Anglia University" in Norwich. The four fatal victims, Dominick Mayor, Jennifer Tebbut, Jaroslav Vacek, and Agnes Silcock, Embry argues, were already implicated in violence and, according to his preliminary judgment, more likely therefore to die violent deaths. Gordon Levine objects to this, since it would imply that the six million victims of the Holocaust in a sense willed their own deaths. Sir Alistair takes the matter under consideration; he is unwilling to foreclose on Embry's rough theorizing, sensing that something valuable may come out of it. But how can he present the case to the faculty board that must approve an extension of Embry's grant? As the novel ends, Ray and Ruby Tebbut are watching the Remembrance Day celebrations on television.

Aldiss's novel, which on the surface ends inconclusively, actually tightens the connections between the reader and the fictional world, for it is there that the answer to the puzzle posed by Embry lies. The reader alone is the privileged observer of the events that led to the catastrophe in Yarmouth. The reader alone has witnessed the subtle interplay of character and circumstance that led each individual to make the choices that would prove fatal to some. Working directly against the postmodern "fictionalizing" of experience, Aldiss reasserts the role of art as a true vehicle of our comprehension of existence. The novel is set above life; in it, life is ordered; through it, we become godlike judge and witness of imaginary events—but these events serve to clarify what is real.

Such a conclusion takes us back to Richard Hughes and *A High Wind in Jamaica,* a famous British novel of 1929, which describes a series of incongruities following on the capture of some apparently innocent children by pirates. As the pirates are about to be condemned to death on grounds that readers of the novel know very well are false, one of the lawyers reflects:

> After all, a criminal lawyer is not concerned with facts, he is concerned with probabilities. It is the novelist who is concerned with facts, whose job it is to say what a particular man did do on a particular occasion: the lawyer does not, cannot be expected to go further than to show what the ordinary man would be most likely to do under presumed circumstances.[18]

In Aldiss's novel, Embry, the social scientist, is working at a disadvantage; he is concerned with probabilities and can never transcend them. Only the novelist can tell us what really happened—and in so doing bestow on the reader a godlike sense of knowledge.

The fourth novel of the Squire Quartet, *Somewhere East of Life,* published in 1994, carries us into the future, well into the twenty-first century. Tom Squire, however, is still alive; he appears fleetingly—as do some of the other characters from the previous novels—as at the end this narrative returns to the Norfolk setting in which Aldiss seems so at home.

Somewhere East of Life, however, for most of its length, carries us into a science fictional world, a future dystopia, in which an illegal industry thrives on stealing human memory. These memories, edited and stored, are sold on an international black market: virtual reality has become the stuff of everyday entertainment. The protagonist, Roy Burnell, is an art expert who works for a huge international organization, World Antiquities and Cultural Heritage (WACH), whose mission is to preserve and catalog cultural treasures. Europe has become united and is prosperous although overpopulated, but there are wars at the fringes, and many parts of the old Soviet empire are in a state of civil war and near anarchy. Burnell seems well-insulated from such troubles until he is betrayed by an old acquaintance, and ten years of his memory are stolen in an illegal Budapest clinic. When he hears that parts of the memory may be recoverable in capsules sold in central Asia, he volunteers for service, first in Georgia, then in Turkmenistan, where his experiences are both horrific and comical. In Georgia he assassinates a local strong man and recovers an important icon of the virgin; in Turkmenistan he vainly seeks for his memory, exploring various stored memory paths without success. Reality gradually fills in some of the missing years and events. His lover, Blanche Bretesche, for whom he betrayed his wife Stephanie, comes back to him and attempts to get him to move to Spain with her. Bur-

nell, however, is obsessed with memories of his wife, who is now married
to a sleazy California businessman, with whom she has had a child. It is
to her that he sends furtive postcards on his journeys, although she has
visited him only once, at the request of a hospital, in order to help him
recover his memory. As Burnell is about to return to Norfolk after his
trip to central Asia, Tom Squire, now the British director of WACH—
and an old friend of the Burnell family—descends on him. This obsessive quest for memory is not altogether wise, Squire tells him: who
would want to have to regain the past at the price of replaying all its
errors and follies in one's mind? Taking an example from opera, Squire
remarks: "It's always a touching moment when Siegfried swallows the
love potion and forgets Brunnhilde in a false passion for Gutrune. One
fears for Siegfried, even while envying him that wholehearted passion."[19]
But who is Brunnhilde in Burnell's life and who is Gutrune? He had
long ago divorced Stephanie, while his relationship with Blanche is ten-
der and passionate although uncommitted.

The novel concludes at Diddisham, the Burnell family home in Norfolk. In the middle of a family reunion, Stephanie arrives and announces
that her husband has managed to buy the capsule with the missing 10
years; she has played it back, entered it and seen Burnell's devotion to
her. She is giving him his memory back, and—her own marriage having
become sterile and meaningless—she is willing to return to him. It
seems, however, that he is unwilling to take her back. He is going to
join Blanche in Madrid. Or is he? The novel ends with a touch of ambiguity, since Burnell simply disappears, and there is the faint possibility
that he has left with Stephanie after all.

Thus the fourth novel of the Squire Quartet ends as tantalizingly—
and in some ways as unsatisfactorily—as the second. Reading it after the
others, however, we are able to grasp something of Aldiss's plan and to
understand some of the ironies of his development as a mainstream novelist. For while in writing the Squire Quartet, Aldiss had seemed to
move away altogether from science fiction, in projecting his characters
forward in time, he is forced to enter a future world that is science fictional in essence. This is precisely the movement visible in Doris Lessing's novel, *The Four-Gated City*, which carries modern life forward until
a science fictional scenario becomes inescapable. The dystopian world of
Somewhere East of Life also certainly reflects the influence of Philip K.
Dick, with Roy Burnell resembling the typical Dick hero, basically honest but wounded by a corrupt world so that his perceptions themselves
are endangered and distorted. Unlike Dick, however, Aldiss seems to

balk at closure, as if fearing that any resolution would somehow falsify reality, which he sees as always ambiguous and open. And this is precisely the case in relation to this novel's many discussions of meaning and values. The God-issue is always alive in Aldiss's novels, but the sensitive and humane characters fall far short of faith; their rational doubt is not merely deconstructive: it alerts them to the fact that existential meaninglessness is intolerable and can only result in a world of corruption and cynicism. Yet, as we see in *Somewhere East of Life,* the faithful are often foolish, narrow, destructive, and morally compromised. The result is a kind of irresolution, underlined by the wide political scope of the later Aldiss novels. History unfolds endless novelties of structure and invention, yet the primitive instincts are by no means hedged in, social chaos threatens, and an authentic life for the individual seems almost out of reach.

Over several decades, Brian Aldiss's mainstream fiction moves from the idyllic to the dystopian, in the end coming close to the implicit assumptions of the science fiction books. In both of the Aldiss fictional worlds, machinery remains an external, extrapolation in time and space solves nothing, and the significant human victories are won by those who fight to hold on to awareness, those who grasp whatever grace is possible from the incomprehensible and beautiful sweep of life, a life that human intelligence—and the good novelist—contemplates as a privileged but often baffled spectator.

Chapter Six

The Short Fiction and the Literary Criticism

If you turn on the light quickly enough, you can see what the darkness looks like.
—Brian Aldiss, Introduction to *A Romance of the Equator* (1989)

The Short Fiction

Since the advent of the science fiction magazines in the 1920s and 1930s, short stories have been the building blocks of almost every repu-tation in the field.[1] But even before the arrival of the pulps and their more respectable successors, many famous writers from Poe and Hawthorne to Fitz-James O'Brien and Edward Bulwer-Lytton used the short narrative as a vehicle for speculative fiction.

This fact is hardly surprising, for one of the key elements in science fiction is the mythos, the structure of the story itself (the so-called verti-cal dimension), which often (although by no means always) overrides the documenting of social interrelationships, the establishing of the created world (the horizontal dimension).[2] Because short fiction works well as myth and science fiction revels in myth, the marriage between the two has often been made in heaven. The central artistic challenge of the speculative story is clear: the writer must establish an unfamiliar, often fantastic, created world while skillfully deploying the narrative itself— he or she must make the vertical and horizontal dimensions function perfectly together. Despite this difficulty, many of the best modern sto-ries have been speculative fiction; yet before the fortunate advent of postmodernism, canonic snobbery or sheer ignorance often excluded them from distinguished mainstream anthologies.

Brian Aldiss has written more than 300 short stories; among these are not many failures, dozens of powerful narratives, and a few that rank as masterpieces. The sheer quantity of Aldiss's output, however, means that any brief survey of his work in this form must content itself with relatively modest objectives. In what follows I shall proceed chronologically, stopping along the way to discuss stories that seem to me important milestones.

Brian Aldiss published his first collection of stories, *Space, Time and Nathaniel,* in 1957, immediately after the successful *Brightfount Diaries.* The publisher was once again Faber & Faber, which, as Aldiss points out in his autobiography, *Bury My Heart at W. H. Smith's,* was probably the only publisher in London that would have been open to such a second book.[3] All of the stories in this collection are worth reading, yet two stand out, "Outside" and "The Failed Men."[4] Aldiss, in fact, thought so well of these that he reprinted them in his collection of *Best SF Stories* (1988). One of the reasons these stories are important is that they go right to the heart of Aldiss's concerns about human nature. "Outside," a simply-told story, almost a parable, deals with the difficulty of discovering what is essentially human. The point of view of the story is given to the alien who is shocked to find that he is not human. At the end he is told: "The inhumanity inside will always give you away . . . However human you are outside."[5]

"Outside" touches on one of the main themes of all of Aldiss's work. It is a story about identity and authenticity. The second important story from the first collection, "The Failed Men" is about the limits of communication; it uses travel into the future to explore one of the possible dead ends of human nature. The Failed Men of the future speak a kind of somber double-talk; their world is a skeletal extrapolation from the overcrowded Singapore of the twenty-fourth century dystopian earth: the successful future of the so-called Paulls, still further ahead in time, is so exalted that it too is incomprehensible. The story suggests—in contrast to most golden-age science fiction—that time solves nothing.

Aldiss's next important story collection, *The Canopy of Time* (1959; published in the United States as *Galaxies Like Grains of Sand,* 1960) contains his most famous story and several others of great interest. It must be noted, however, that Aldiss's unified plan for this volume, modeled on Ray Bradbury's *The Illustrated Man,* was rather butchered by both his American and British publishers.[6] While the British edition was published with no linking narrative and with added stories, the American edition, although it retained the linking narrative, changed the order of the stories and dropped several. Despite this, both collections are excellent. Aldiss's stories span the whole of our galaxy's future, and when read in proper sequence, provide a disturbing yet intriguing glimpse of human fate. Despite the unified scope of the overall narra-

tive, each story is quite different from its companions and each introduces new characters and issues.

"All the World's Tears," for example, is one of the best Brian Aldiss
stories. Set in a forty-fourth century dystopian earth, it dramatizes the
frustration of human passion (a mating Council implants explosives in
humans to discourage contact) amid a failed earth ecology—and yet it is
witty, inventive, and terribly funny.

"Who Can Replace a Man?" is Aldiss's most reprinted story, one trans-
lated into many languages and familiar even to readers who know nothing
of Aldiss's other work.[7] Here, civilization has dwindled to a handful of
people, and intelligent robots do nearly all the work. One day a radio-
operator robot fails to receive his work instructions and the complex interaction between the machines breaks down. When some of them gather
together to discuss what has occurred, a natural hierarchy is formed as
they establish what class brain each of them possesses. The robots believe
humanity has died out and decide to assume control and to restore the
now nonproductive society to proper functioning. Finding this task not so
easy, they head south toward the deserted badlands, where they intend to
establish a new order. They arrive after a weeklong journey to discover a
small group of degraded and impoverished humans living in a cave. One
of these, an old man, promptly orders the robots to find them some food.
The machines reply: "Yes, Master . . . immediately!"[8]

This masterpiece of short fiction wastes not a word in turning the
machine threat on its head, yet the story is ironic: human mastery,
attested to even by incomparably powerful semiconscious machines, is
seen to have resulted in the degradation of humanity, in an ecologically
despoiled earth.

"Poor Little Warrior," not actually collected in either of the books
mentioned above, appeared in *The Magazine of Fantasy and Science Fiction*
in April 1958, and was reprinted in Aldiss's *Best SF Stories* in 1965. This
story is one of Aldiss's most stunningly beautiful prose poems, themati-
cally simple and yet breathtaking in its use of language. A time-travel
story, it describes the Jurassic expedition of a human hunter who is simply overwhelmed by the alien world, which is both monstrous and
impossibly dangerous. Aldiss's scatological predilection is incorporated
here and serves the powerful realism of this outlandish and memorable
fantasy. The story resembles Thurber rather than Ray Bradbury or
Arthur C. Clarke and can be related to Aldiss's suggestion that science
fiction depicts "hubris clobbered by nemesis."

Another memorable story appeared in *The Airs of Earth: Science Fiction Stories* (1963). "Old Hundredth" tells of a future earth taken over by intelligent but nonhuman creatures—among them, sloths, bears, and dolphins. This tale creates a fantastic Salvador Dali landscape where living things may be transported into shimmering columns of light that sing. The protagonist, Dadi, a giant slothlike female creature, at the end is thus transported, and the song she chooses to become is the famous hymn with the words carefully pointed: "All creatures that on earth do dwell . . ." In this story the emphasis shifts away from the human; the reader is drawn sympathetically into the contemplation of other life-forms, which are given a sacred dimension by the famous hymn referred to in the title. The story is, however, not quite artistically perfect, since here Aldiss visibly labors to establish the horizontal dimension of his created world.

When we turn to *The Moment of Eclipse* (1970), published by Faber & Faber, we see Aldiss's stories moving toward mainstream, while reflecting also the influence of the new wave. Clearly, none of these pieces suffers from the pretentiousness and self-indulgence that marred too many of the stories that appeared in Michael Moorcock's *New Worlds*. Even so—and although one can understand Aldiss's need to move on—this later work represents no particular improvement over his first manner. The title story, for example, tells of a filmmaker who pursues an ideal woman to Africa, catches up with her in Europe, only to fail in the moment preceding the intended act of consummation, "the moment of eclipse." A story about art, the piece seems more chic than powerful, very cultivated, but a little too intellectual in a peculiarly sixties manner. (Compare, for example, the 1963 Godard film *Contempt*, which is also about filmmaking—and similarly cerebral). Other stories in *The Moment of Time*, such as, "The Day we Embarked for Cythera," "Working in the Spaceship Yards," and "Swastika," for all their cool competence, lack heart. This newer leaner mode had been anticipated by "Man on Bridge" and "Girl and Robot With Flowers" (both of which had appeared in earlier collections); on the other hand, Aldiss's attempt to recapture his earlier imaginative flights in "The Worm that Flies," results in a turgid and overwrought piece in which he almost seems to be parodying himself.

The two most powerful stories in *The Moment of Eclipse* are "Super-Toys Last All Summer Long" and "Heresies of the Huge God," both of which rank high among Aldiss's short narratives.[9] "Super Toys" has some links with the novel *Greybeard*, but it is *Greybeard* by way of Philip K. Dick and the sixties flash mod scene. A simple, powerful story, it evokes a whole present-future world of facade and fakery in a few pages. Nor does its rapier-like satire prevent the ending from catching the reader's breath: what appeared to be the tragedy of a neglected, isolated child and mother turns out to be the pathos of human-machine relationship in a civilization that has closed the gap between flesh and the inventions of flesh in all ways but one. The missing link is love and the story ends with a devastating irony that encompasses both hope and hopelessness.

"Heresies of the Huge God" is old-fashioned mainstream science fiction, but with a satirical thrust and objectivity worthy of the best of Stanislaw Lem. The huge god is a kind of mechanical bug of enormous dimensions, which, for no reason known to humanity, lands on the earth and smashes and rearranges the geography. A fanatic religious movement seeks to placate this "god," and the story is told by one of its adherents. In fact, the god has left once before; as the story unfolds we learn it has been gone for 10 years, although not before deflecting the earth away from the sun and turning it into a freezing hell. The story encompasses several classic science fiction themes and devices, for example, the helplessness of the earth in the face of space-invasion; the idea that a change of scale would reveal the weaknesses of society; the notion that human crisis must result in failed communication. Here Aldiss's control of tone is not perfect: in two or three places the priestly account lapses into a kind of Monty Python self-kidding. If this lapse were carried any further, the whole narrative would disintegrate. Nonetheless, "Heresies of the Huge God" is an unforgettable story.

Last Orders and Other Stories, published by Jonathan Cape in 1977, is mainstream science fiction. The level of this collection is very high: the stories are terse, often grim, but with an underlying stoical humor that renders catastrophe and human failure in a knowing way that stops well short of cynicism. In the title story, for example, the earth and the moon suffer an apocalyptic destruction. A no-nonsense military man from a rescue party, after a few drinks, opts to stay with two survivors who are reluctant to be airlifted out. They end up establishing a kind of pub-rapport, dialoguing about trivia while the world literally crumbles around them. In "An Appearance of Life," from the same collection, a future researcher activates the holograms of two married lovers who have been dead for centuries. They exchange the touching and absolutely true-to-life regrets and reassurances of any such couple; then the researcher (to whom the ancient customs of love are quaint) realizes that their comments originate from different periods in their lives and that the dialogue is only apparently authentic, since it runs in a loop and begins again where it started. Here, Aldiss's mature perspective carries him past satirical exposure to elegiac reflection on the futile but somehow touching requirements of our contemporary versions of marital love.

In *New Arrivals, Old Encounters: Twelve Stories* (1979), we find one of Aldiss's most endearing and poetically resonant tales, "The Small Stones of Tu Fu." In this masterly and effortlessly delivered vignette we visit the eighth century A.D., the China of the great poet Tu Fu. The story unfolds from the point of view of a Stapledonian-like supreme intelligence who roves through time and plays a divine game with the stones of the world, arranging them by size and number. But Tu Fu, just before his death on a Yangtze riverboat, gives him one special stone, together with a poem, and the intelligent and godlike visitor eventually confesses his ironically framed but genuine affection for mankind—and for "the immortal river of Tu Fu's thought."[10] Art connects with spirit and redeems the world from abstraction and mere number.

In *Seasons in Flight* (1984), Aldiss continued his movement in the direction of pseudofolktale and parable. Here he achieves some of his most perfect stories. "A Romance of the Equator" is a faultless parable about love crystalline and profound—though lightly delivered. (The story is very much from the male perspective; one feels that it deserves an equally poetic response from a woman writer.) In "The Blue Background," a tale of Slovakia from the same collection, a photographer visits an obscure village where a young peasant shows him an ancient image of Christ set against a blue background. The photographer takes the picture, and years later, after the church and the icon have been destroyed, he sends his photograph to the peasant boy who showed him where to find the icon. The young peasant, grown to manhood and already disillusioned, is disappointed: the photograph is in sepia and fails to show the blue background "the glimpse of infinity" that he had loved "before life closed in."[11] This story represents another peak of Aldiss's storytelling and once again affirms the power of art to give perspective to onrushing human existence.

Aldiss's later stories have been enormously diverse. One thinks of the too-obvious but occasionally biting "My Country 'Tis Not Only of Thee," in which Britain becomes Vietnam. America invades: a line is established at the Cotswolds between the "commie" north and the collaborative south; Ireland (Cambodia) is bombed and dissenters are shot by irritable Yankee soldiers.[12] Here, however, the implausibility of the parallel undermines the effectiveness of the satire. Much more frightening and trenchant are the "Gothic" stories, which, although occasionally laced with wild humor, darkly hint at weird sex, witchcraft, and domination—"Lies," "North Scarning," "Infestation," and "How an Inner Door Opened to my Heart," are examples of these stories, which all date from the mid-eighties. Sharing some qualities with the "Gothic" stories but more related to his classic science fiction stories is Aldiss's "You Never Asked My Name" (1985). This astonishing tale has everything— action, psychology, perversity, terror. In it, a powerful warrior guard enters into a painful and near-purgative dialogue with an android female. He is not quite transformed—in fact, in none of the stories just mentioned are the various and necessary character transformations really achieved. No macho posturing afflicts Aldiss's work: he has always been most enlightened on the subject of male and female, yet all of the stories cited above reflect a new and painful awareness of the difficulties that mark the changes in the power-relationship between the sexes in recent decades.

Brian Aldiss's short stories are among his best works of any kind. First of all, their range is extraordinary, testifying to the writer's open-minded curiosity about human life, society, mechanisms, time, and space. Second, in these stories Aldiss almost always solves with ease the basic problem of the science fiction and fantasy narrative: that of reconciling the vertical dimension of story with the horizontal dimension of world. Third, Aldiss's chameleon-like stylistics are here a positive factor; he is almost always able to match his style of storytelling to the subject at hand. Thus, the Aldiss stories, taken all in all, have nearly everything: humor, intelligence, imagination, insight, poetry, analysis, pathos, and terror. Very seldom are they merely clever; even more rarely are they unfocused or clumsy.

In the Brian Aldiss short stories, written over several decades, one can see a development, a movement first of all from science fiction as fable to a more traditional kind of fable (influenced certainly by Aldiss's travels). On the other hand, most of Aldiss's later stories, however much they play with generic conventions, are character-based in a powerful way. One can see an extension of range from science fictional themes (space, time, machinery, social evolution) to themes that are much more traditional: the spells of love, human cruelty, memory, the power of art. Aldiss's later stories, however, unlike his later long fiction, have not broken contact with the science fiction world altogether. They continually return to earlier themes, mixing modes and changing perspectives in ways that are surprising and nearly always pleasing.

Given his range and output, his consistent mastery, and his ability to focus on the essentials of the human condition, Brian Aldiss must be considered not only one of the best writers of short speculative fiction, but one of the significant British short story writers of the century.

Anthologies and Critical Works

Just as the short story has always been the chief building block of science fiction reputations, so the science fiction anthology has been—at least since the 1940s and 1950s—the medium by which ambitious editors have hoped to establish contact with new readers.[13] Many anthologists—especially in the earlier days—seemed to cherish the hope of legitimizing the ancestry of science fiction; they also wanted to break down the boundaries between the genre and mainstream and avant-garde literature, a process that in fact would end up being much more complex than they dreamed. Dedicated readers of science fiction, on the other hand, have always favored anthologies that emphasize the clubbish nature of their membership in fandom; they like anthologies in which editors and writers surround the stories with commentary and chatty *obiter scripta* on practically any subject—the printed and bound equivalent of a science fiction convention and an inheritance of the garrulous exchanges in the old pulps. Dedicated science fiction readers have also preferred anthologies with themes—"the end of the world," for example, or "first contact"—or stories drawn from the issues of a favorite magazine.

Influential early collections of science fiction include both kinds of anthology. *Adventures in Time and Space* (1946), edited by Raymond J. Healy and J. Francis McComas, derived mostly from John W. Campbell's *Astounding.* Fletcher Pratt's 1951 *World of Wonder,* in contrast, ranged widely into fantasy and includes both Kipling and Kafka. August Derleth's *Beyond Time and Space* (1950), also struggled for roots; it included Thomas More and Rabelais as well as Heinlein and Bradbury. Groff Conklin's various anthologies, notably the very Campbellian *Possible Worlds of Science Fiction* (1951), were orientated to fandom.[14]

When Brian Aldiss himself became an anthologist in 1961, he made few radical departures from the approaches of his predecessors, although he did introduce several unknown American writers to the British public. Nonetheless, Aldiss's *Penguin Science Fiction* (1961) seems to have struck just the right note. The sales were impressive and similar collections followed in 1963 and 1964—all three were bound together in *The*

Science Fiction Omnibus of 1973.[15] The 24 stories in the three collections are all mainstream science fiction and they include pieces by Simak, Asimov, Clarke, and Ballard, as well as stories by John Steinbeck and Howard Fast. Each volume has an introduction by Aldiss: the 1961 collection contains the famous statement: "Science fiction is no more written for scientists than ghost stories are written for ghosts"—a quip (repeated in the introduction to *Billion Year Spree*) that demonstrates Aldiss's skill at reassuring potential readers about the genre.[16] In the introduction to the Omnibus he writes: "Throughout the genre, since the beginning, nemesis has clobbered hubris."[17] Generally speaking, however, Aldiss lets the stories speak for themselves, avoiding analysis and also the garrulous, cultish, and often self-promoting commentaries which, as I have indicated, many science fiction editors wrap around their chosen selections. (The apex of this latter kind of editing probably occurred in Harlan Ellison's *Dangerous Visions* of 1967, which is nonetheless an important anthology and comparable to Aldiss's in literary quality.)[18]

From this auspicious beginning in the 1960s Aldiss went on over the next three decades to compile a remarkable number of entertaining and literate anthologies. *Best Fantasy Stories* of 1962 included work by Saki and Lernet-Holenia; *Introducing SF* (1964), published by Faber, was mainstream science fiction. More experimental in conception were Aldiss's collaborations with Harry Harrison, including *Best SF: 1967–75*, and the decadal anthologies: *Decade, the 1940s* (1975); *Decade, the 1950s* (1976); and *Decade, the 1960s* (1977). Aldiss's own thematic and historical anthologies are imaginative and sometimes provocative: these latter include anthologies of "way back when futures" which featured some of the well-tried "golden age" themes or subgenres: space opera (1974), space odysseys (1975), evil earths (1975), galactic empires (1976), and perilous planets (1978). On each of these subgenres and stories Aldiss had perceptive comments.

The Aldiss anthologies were well-received by both science fiction fandom and by the general reading public. The case of *Billion Year Spree*, his major critical-historical study, published in 1973, was quite different. In *The Detached Retina*, Aldiss himself has discussed its reception at length, and with his usual humor and objectivity. There he tells us that "few reviewers stood up in support of my arguments in *Billion Year Spree*"— and names some of his detractors.[19] He goes on to describe the circumstances under which the book was written and recalls his aims in undertaking it, namely, to define science fiction as a genre and to "place" it in the general literary-historical context. This meant, as Aldiss explains, taking it out of the hands of the "gadgeteers" and demolishing at last the absurd notion of science fiction fandom that Hugo Gernsback was the genre's only true progenitor. Aldiss plausibly sought science fiction's roots in Mary Shelley's *Frankenstein* (written in 1816 and published in 1818), although he was certainly not the first to do so.[20] Those, like the present writer, who were eager to construct academic courses in science fiction in the early 1970s under the watchful eyes of suspicious faculty committees, commonly turned for authentication either to the respectable Thomas More, to Mary Shelley, or else to Poe, depending upon whether they wished to connect science fiction to Utopian thought or preferred to relate the genre to the cultural crisis connected with the massive social and intellectual changes that were already half-visible at the beginning of the nineteenth century. *Frankenstein* is clearly one of the founding texts of science fiction, which is not to say it is not also a Gothic tale, a philosophical romance, and other things as well (a point Aldiss has often made, and which he concedes to excellent academic analysts such as David Ketterer).

In retrospect, *Billion Year Spree* (revised, with David Wingrove, as *Trillion Year Spree,* and given a Hugo Award in 1987) is arguably among the best books of its kind ever published—whether we understand its kind to be "generic history" or literary history for the nonspecialist general reader. Aldiss's book is more useful and much more readable than J. O. Bailey's pioneering *Pilgrims Through Space and Time* (1947), which appeared before most contemporary science fiction was even published. There are many good analyses of individual genres but no comparably brilliant and balanced history of any genre, none, for example, of Gothic literature, the detective story, the spy story, or the horror tale, despite the existence of many books on these subjects, including some by famous names. One only has to compare the Aldiss book with H. P. Lovecraft's *Supernatural Horror in Literature,* Ford Madox Ford's *The March of Literature,* or J. B. Priestley's *The Literature of Western Man,* to see how great is Aldiss's achievement, for he is much more comprehensive and less eccentric than Lovecraft, more inclusive and focused than Ford, and infinitely superior to Priestley in his ability to discern patterns and to pinpoint the strengths and weaknesses of individual authors and books. There are numerous memorable moments in Aldiss's survey, which is brilliantly organized so as to begin with Mary Shelley and to work chronologically backward, to deal with Poe, Voltaire, Swift, and Lucian before taking up the Victorians and Jules Verne. Aldiss moves between serious literature and the pulp fiction of Edgar Rice Burroughs with ease and humor; he has the measure equally of Olaf Stapledon and C. S. Lewis; understands well the relationship of the magazines and fandom to the development of science fiction; holds social and scientific developments reasonably in focus; gives us a clear account of the arrival of the new wave, and produces new perspectives on both "the power drive" implicit in Campbellian fiction and on the mainstream writers—Poe, Kafka, Huxley, Orwell—who at one point formed the only available links between science fiction and serious literary study.

Perhaps the best way of demonstrating the deftness and originality of Aldiss's account is to quote a few of his remarks on George Orwell's *1984*—a dystopia, to be sure, but one of the favorite pieces of token science fiction mentioned—and taught in courses—in pre-Aldiss days. In *Billion Year Spree* Aldiss reads Orwell's most famous book "inside-out," that is, from the perspective of the science fiction genre, and from that point of view, proceeds to deeper insights:

> It is entirely on the cards that Orwell, with his love of the outlawed in literature, read a lot of science fiction. His *1984* reads rather like a lobotomized Van Vogt, with its Newspeak standing in for Van Vogt's General Semantics. The thought police and the whole psychotic plot of the solitary good guy against the universe is pure Van Vogt, the twist in the tail being that in Orwell's case the universe, represented by Big Brother, wins. Perhaps Winston Smith's attempts to unravel the past reflect some past Orwellian attempt to unravel The World of Nul-a.
>
> To say this is partly to poke fun at the legions of learned commentators who find *1984* a nest of stolen ideas. For the novel possesses two cardinal virtues, one intellectual and one emotional, which, taken together, make an original contribution to the debate.
>
> Firstly, Orwell states clearly that the object of a party in power is to hold power. His Party holds power and glories in it; hence that memorable line, "If you want a picture of the future, think of a boot stamping on the human face forever." Unlike his predecessors, unlike even Wells—forever on his way up—Orwell identified strongly with the lower classes, even when he found them repulsive; and from this viewpoint, he saw lucidly that those who are down are kept down. It is this perception which makes Brave New World seem namby-pamby; for Huxley, secure in the upper classes, never thinks to give us a sight of the whip.
>
> The emotional virtue of *1984* is that Orwell's utopian desires are so much more human than those of his greater predecessors, of Plato, More and the others. His recipe for a good life is tender and fallen: something to eat, no nosey neighbours, a bit of comfort, and a girl to take to bed. (254–55)

This passage may cause some readers, recalling Orwell's essays, to conclude that Aldiss's inimitable style is in fact not far removed from Orwell's own sharply etched discursive prose. Few general histories of literature achieve such brilliance of insight at any point; *Billion Year Spree* has things as good on nearly every page.

Billion Year Spree is beyond question the most valuable overview of science fiction yet produced, and much of Aldiss's success in documenting the development of his favorite genre arises from his being able to maintain an objective distance from it. This success has led to his often being accepted as an authority in a field that rarely accepts consensus. In 1979 Universal studios employed Aldiss as an advisor to defend the film *Battlestar Galactica* against an action for plagiarism brought on by Lucasfilm and Fox concerning the movie *Star Wars*. Aldiss, having already compiled an anthology of classic space operas, was able to demonstrate that the basic elements of both movies had been devised long before either film had been made. When Aldiss was asked by a lawyer what his initial response to Star Wars had been he responded, "I experienced the delights of recognition."[21] The suit against Universal studios was soon dropped. Aldiss's ability to step back and examine the science fiction genre from various external vantage points may well explain his ability to consistently renew his art in a manner that few others have achieved.

Brian Aldiss has produced criticism in various forms. One must read not only *Billion Year Spree* but also *The Shape of Further Things, The Detached Retina,* the prefaces to the various anthologies, as well as Aldiss's autobiographical works, to get the full range of his criticism of science fiction. What kind of critic is he? What does he see as the central values of literature in general?

First of all, Aldiss is no systematic critic with a single large idea; he is a fox, not a hedgehog. Nonetheless, some consistent values emerge. First, he writes as an old-fashioned humanist, one of a vanishing breed. Literature must portray as accurately as possible our imperfect human world. We live inside nature but are also capable of being detached from it. This detachment makes it possible to create art. Yet because of that same power of detachment, our sympathies often dry up; we become mechanical. For the writer, it is the worst of fates, because the writer's real subject is men and women, not machinery, social systems, and theories. Literature portrays a fallen humanity; perfection is out of reach, is probably not even desirable, and striving for it, or even for consistent pleasures, for escape from suffering, we become comic or tragic in our turn. Morality is central to literature, and Aldiss understands morality as the writer's power to differentiate between honesty and sham, between the authentic human gesture and the mechanical or self-serving one. Morality is also determined by how well the writer understands the claims of all life, the fragility and preciousness of many living forms, as well as the impersonal and terrifying power of boundless nature. The writer must not narrow his or her vision too much; breadth of perception counts for much. What also counts are two qualities we can read in the Aldiss perspective, qualities he never quite names, but for all his humor and deftness of touch, he seems to affirm: the first is what Arnold Bennett saw as the writer's capacity for a "Christlike compassion," and the second, Rebecca West described as "the completest omniscience about human nature."[22] Aldiss's criticism—for all its tolerance, its modesty, and its ripples of incisive humor—shows him to be in search of such ideals and always sensitive as to how the writer is embodying such love and knowledge in the form of the work.

Conclusion

As we move forward into a new millennium, science fiction seems more oddly placed than ever within the general culture. True, the reader exploring any of the large general bookstores in North America inevitably finds a section devoted to "science fiction and fantasy," yet the shelves in question are likely to be dominated by legions of fantasy chroniclers following bravely in the wake of The *Lord of the Rings*. Gaudy covers abound, heralding items marketed under such rubrics as "Volume VI" of the "Mists of Time" series, "the best since Tolkien," in which the reader is promised a "startlingly new" hero or heroine, not to mention the delight of exploring kingdoms dubbed with names like Gullibal or Quagmere. Many of the shelves will carry spin-offs from the Star Trek or Star Wars series or novels written by astronauts, actors, or Isaac Asimov. Here and there, visible among the riot of garish color, the reader may well find a familiar classic or two, John Wyndham's *The Day of the Triffids* or Walter Miller Jr.'s *A Canticle for Leibowitz,* yet most of the works that informed critics would consider milestones of the science fiction genre will be missing, including probably all of Brian Aldiss's. While the situation might be different in the more specialized science fiction bookstores, key classics will be unavailable there too, including probably most of Brian Aldiss's fiction. Meanwhile, although television is serving up endless replays of Every Science Fiction Series and Film Ever Made, you may wait a long time to see *La Jetée, Solaris*, or *The Quartermass Experiment.*

Even though, increasingly, university students are taking courses in science fiction and postmodernism, writing Ph.D. dissertations on the relationship between the Campbellian editorship and the science fiction stories of the forties, or deconstructing Obi-Wan Kenobi, critics will tell you that mystery fiction, the thriller novel, or the horror tale are the genres of the moment. Analysts of social trends suggest that the public has lost interest in the challenge of space and thus in science fiction. Were the Voyageur photographs of bleak planets and barren satellites just too daunting for a public accustomed to little green men and faces on Mars? Does science's beleaguered but still intact "objectivity" condemn it to irrelevance in an age of ideologies and irrational commitments? Has the science fiction genre been swallowed up by postmodernism? Are we never to acquire a science fiction tradition that is consistent, well-defined, stable, and secure?

The drift of these melancholy observations and questions does lead us back to the question of Brian Aldiss's fate as a writer. Is it possible that Brian Aldiss is condemned to be regarded as merely a science fiction writer in an age that is increasingly unsympathetic to his kind of science fiction? It may be so, yet this conclusion, even if it were true, would falsify and unduly narrow Brian Aldiss's achievement. For Aldiss is also, as this survey of his work attempts to show, a significant writer of mainstream fiction, an interesting experimenter with a flare for postmodern narrative, an outstanding literary historian, and one of the most intelligent and incisive essayists ever to write about the science fiction and fantasy genres. This versatility itself, however, raises questions.

In his autobiography, *Bury My Heart at W. H. Smith's,* Aldiss records an incident connected with the marketing of his mainstream novel, *Forgotten Life,* by his agent Clarissa Rushdie.

> *Forgotten Life* was my first book to have a Canadian publisher. The Canadian publishing industry is flourishing, but—like Australia—has a struggle disentangling itself from rival American and British markets. Canadian rights were traditionally taken either by American or British publishers.
>
> My agent cut the knot, reserving my Canadian rights and auctioning the book in Canada. Eight publishers were involved in the auction. Seven swore they liked the novel greatly but thought that since my name was too well-known as an SF writer, a "straight" novel would be difficult to promote. Only Doubleday Canada had the courage to buy it.
>
> This news was phoned to me by Clarissa. We discussed it, I professed myself satisfied and she rang off. After an hour, she rang back.
>
> "Brian, you sounded so disappointed with the Canadian offer. If you don't think the money's sufficient, I could ring Gollancz and see if they would buy Canadian rights for a little more."
>
> It was good of her to be so concerned. But I never worry over money. . . . What hit me was the thought that, after thirty years of my campaigning, people still think in these rigidly confining categories. I had just been turned down by seven competing publishers because I wrote SF. (*Bury My Heart,* 186–87)

This seemingly trivial anecdote touches on a large issue raised by Brian Aldiss's writing career. For Aldiss is nearly unique among creative artists in that the nature of his production has almost hopelessly fractured his potential audience. Let me be clear on this issue. There are of course many examples of versatile artists and writers who have written a diversity of works and who have appealed to various audiences. Academics like C. S. Lewis and J. I. M. Stewart have written both scholarly books and popular novels. George Gershwin wrote "serious" works and also popular shows and songs. Erich Wolfgang Korngold wrote both operas and film music. Kurt Vonnegut has written both mainstream and science fiction works. Martin Scorsese has made movies as diverse as *Raging Bull* and *The Age of Innocence.* None of these analogies, however, quite covers the case of Brian Aldiss. For unlike C. S. Lewis or J. I. M. Stewart, Brian Aldiss's achievement almost completely resides in his fiction. Unlike the situation of Gershwin and Korngold, there is no easy stylistic bridge from one audience to another and no career path that smooths the transition. Kurt Vonnegut, for all his talent, has not created equally significant work in both science fiction and mainstream fiction, while the work of Martin Scorsese is rescued from too much diversity by the traditional license of the film auteur to venture across genre boundaries.

Brian Aldiss's case is very different from the other creators just mentioned. His talent and diversity of interests have led him to produce almost equally interesting work for two sharply divided audiences, the serious science fiction audience, which was always a minority of science fiction readers and which today seems to be shrinking further, and a mainstream audience that—thanks to his intermittent and sometimes inconsistent production—has no clear sense of his work.

It may not be a happy thought, but it is a truism that career focus and consistency of development do affect a writer's chances of being accepted as a significant force by his or her contemporaries. They may also affect a writer's place in history. One can imagine a future in which the wall that seems to divide the two worlds of Brian Aldiss, the science fiction world and the mainstream world, will be broken down. But honesty compels the observation that no such world exists now, nor can one see anything resembling such a world on the horizon, given the relation of the writer to marketing and audience factors in view today.

In the preceding chapters I have made a long journey through almost all of Brian Aldiss's significant writings and have attempted to evaluate them afresh, venturing to challenge those familiar with Aldiss's work with a revised canon, while at the same time aiming to inspire investigation on the part of readers who may have shunned Aldiss because they were daunted by his sheer productivity or because they feared to find the stale body of a played-out tradition embalmed in his pages.

The most successful Brian Aldiss science fiction novels include *Non-Stop, Hothouse, Greybeard, The Saliva Tree, The Eighty-Minute Hour, Moreau's Other Island,* and the *Helliconia* series, the latter being among the monumental works of twentieth-century science fiction. Aldiss has been equally successful as a short story writer; arguably, he has written more good science fiction stories than anyone, and several of his stories would hardly be out of place in an anthology of the best short tales of any kind of the past 50 years. Aldiss's history of science fiction, *Billion Year Spree,* will always be given credit for having refocused attention on the science fiction genre in a way that suggests its true nature and history; at the same time, whatever the changes in literary fashions, the book will endure as one of those rare, eternally readable literary commentaries and take its place on the shelf beside Chesterton's *The Victorian Age in Literature,* Forster's *Aspects of the Novel,* and Gilbert Highet's *Poets in a Landscape,* books about literature that have wit and charm as well as truth. *Bury My Heart at W. H. Smith's* has a similar readability and is one of the most deft modern literary autobiographies.

Although it is as a science fiction writer that he will be best remembered, Brian Aldiss's very good mainstream fiction will certainly survive and be read as an accurate chronicle of its age. The embarrassment of the *Horatio Stubbs Saga* will be forgotten and *The Squire Quartet,* despite its almost perverse lack of unity, will find readers who will appreciate its thoroughgoing humanism, and its sharp perspective on life in the West in the twentieth century.

The conclusion must be that Brian Aldiss is one of the major science fiction writers of the century but also something more. Exactly what that "something more" consists of depends not only on the evaluations of critics but on the responses of audiences yet to come, audiences that can more readily dispense with literary categories and take on the challenge of reading books from a single author that are diverse, probing, and good simply on their own terms.

Notes and References

Chapter One

1. Autobiographical statements are scattered through Brian Aldiss's nonfiction works, but three main sources are: *Bury My Heart at W. H. Smith's: A Writing Life* (London: Hodder & Stoughton, 1990)—a full-length autobiography that deals mostly with his literary career; "A Walk in the Glass Forest," in Margaret Aldiss, *The Work of Brian W. Aldiss: An Annotated Bibliography and Guide,* ed. Boden Clarke (San Bernardino, Calif.: R. Reginald, Borgo Press, 1992), 320–48—a brief but vivid evocation of his childhood; and "Magic and Bare Boards," in Brian Aldiss and Harry Harrison, *Hell's Cartographers* (London: Weidenfeld & Nicolson, SF Horizons, 1975), 173–209—a piece that begins evocatively and ends with some general comments on SF and the present era.

2. Frank Hatherley, ed., *A is For Brian*: *A 65th Birthday Present for Brian W. Aldiss from his Family, Friends, Colleagues, and Admirers* (London: Avernus, 1990), 14.

3. Hatherley, *A is For Brian,* 14.

4. Hatherley, *A is for Brian,* 117.

5. "I had married in 1948. By 1958, my wife and I had nothing much to say to each other, and only boredom to communicate" ("A Walk in the Glass Forest," 330). "Margaret and I recognized each other from our first meeting, which meant that we could stand a lot of mutual nonsense, and do so even with an amount of pleasure" (*Hell's Cartographers,* 197).

6. Linda Fleming, "The American SF Sub-culture." *Science Fiction Studies* 4, pt. 3 (November 1977): 263–71.

7. Harry Martinson, *Aniara*: *A Review of Man in Time and Space* (New York: Avon, 1956). I was fortunate to see Karl-Birger Blomdahl's operatic setting of this striking poem in Hamburg in 1960. There are many connections with the mood of the Aldiss novel, but both versions of Aniara are much grimmer.

8. On "social science fiction" see Donald Lawler, *Approaches to Science Fiction* (Boston: Houghton Mifflin, 1978), 465–66.

9. Brian Griffin and David Wingrove, *Apertures: A Study of the Writings of Brian Aldiss,* Contributions to the Study of Science Fiction & Fantasy, no. 8 (Westport, Conn.: Greenwood Press, 1984), 81.

10. Judith Merril, ed., *England Swings SF* (New York: Ace, 1968), 278–82.

11. Aldiss, *The Detached Retina: Aspects of Science Fiction and Fantasy* (Syracuse, N.Y.: Syracuse University Press, 1995), 24.

12.   "Unreal Estates" (A conversation between Brian Aldiss, C. S. Lewis, and Kingsley Amis) in *Spectrum 4,* ed. Kingsley Amis and Robert Conquest (New York: Berkley, 1965), 9–17.

13.   Colin Greenland, *The Entropy Exhibition: Michael Moorcock and the British "New Wave" in Science Fiction* (London: Routledge & Kegan Paul, 1983), 51–68.

14.   Mary Shelley, *Frankenstein, or The Modern Prometheus,* ed. James Rieger (1818; reprint, Indianapolis: Bobbs-Merril, 1974). The Waldman passage is in the first, or 1818, version of the text. "They" (the modern scientists, according to M. Waldman) "ascend into the heavens; they have discovered how the blood circulates, and the nature of the air we breathe. They have acquired new and almost unlimited powers; they can command the thunders of heaven, mimic the earthquake, and even mock the invisible world with its own shadows" (Shelley, *Frankenstein,* 42).

15.   Carl D. Malmgren, *Worlds Apart* (Indianapolis: Indiana University Press, 1991), 8.

16.   Malmgren, *Worlds Apart,* 10.

17.   Ron Goulart, *An Informal History of the Pulp Magazines* (New York: Ace, 1972), and David Wingrove, *The Science Fiction Source Book* (New York: Van Nostrand-Reinhold, 1984), 274–81.

18.   Brian W. Aldiss, *Billion Year Spree: The True History of Science Fiction* (Garden City, N.Y.: Doubleday,, 1973), 209–12.

19.   Aldiss, *Billion Year Spree,* 215–43.

20.   Sam J. Lundwall (*Science Fiction: What It's All About* [New York: Ace, 1971], 240–41) quotes Campbell himself in the act of demolishing this fan-centered glorification of the past.

21.   "The New Wave discovered the miraculous present," as Aldiss wrote in *Bury My Heart,* 130.

22.   Kingsley Amis, introduction to *The Golden Age of Science Fiction* (London: Hutchinson, 1981).

23.   The marketing of mass-audience books is often a key in these matters. The most recent edition of Philip K. Dick's *Valis* (New York: Vintage, 1995), for example, features a quotation from Ursula K. Le Guin, which refers to Dick as "our own home-grown Borges," something that would have been unthinkable a few decades earlier, even assuming that Borges had been well-known to the general American science fiction reader at that point.

24.   For more on these distinctions, see Malmgren, *Worlds Apart,* 12.

25.   For more on this aspect of science fiction, see Wingrove, *Science Fiction Source Book,* 54–55.

26.   In discussing *Hothouse,* for example, Brian Griffin invokes the following names: Wordsworth, Shelley, Byron, Kokoschka, Joyce, Wells, Stapledon, Shakespeare, Ibsen, C. S. Lewis, Louis MacNeice, R. D. Laing, and Whitman—and this approach is quite typical for these writers, who constantly

tempt the reader's skepticism by surrounding even Aldiss's moderately successful texts with such illustrious reference points (Griffin and Wingrove, *Apertures,*
41–55).

Chapter Two

1.   Michael R. Collings, *Brian W. Aldiss* (Mercer Island, Wash.: Starmont House, 1986), 9. Collings downplays the connection with Heinlein. But
see Aldiss and Harrison, *Hell's Cartographers,* 191.

2.   "*Non-Stop* is one of the finest traditional SF novels ever written, a
story with a concealed environment, full of plot moves and surprising revelations, all about science and its consequences for the universe and human
nature" (Christopher Priest, in Hatherley, *A is for Brian,* 79).

3.   Collings discounts the importance of the change of title, on the
grounds that Roy Complain's discovery that he is on a starship is not the central
focus of the novel (Collings, *Brian W. Aldiss,* 9). For another view, see Richard
Mathews, *Aldiss Unbound: The Science Fiction of Brian W. Aldiss* (San Bernardino,
Calif.: Borgo Press, 1977), 8.

4.   Frederic Jameson carefully connects the shifting realities of the plot,
that is, Aldiss's manipulation of the reader, with the novel's ultimate and most
important theme, the manipulation of human beings by others or by a political
system. Frederic Jameson, "Generic Discontinuities in SF: Brian W. Aldiss's
Starship," *Science Fiction Studies* 1, no. 2 (Fall 1973): 59.

5.   Complain's mounting anger and his inability to find a satisfying
view of existence may be compared to the anger-become-cynicism of the
"Angry Young Men" of 1950s Britain (see Aldiss and Harrison, *Hell's Cartographers,* 189). Aldiss describes the starship itself as both a metaphor of personal
entrapment and an image suggesting "the way in which technology without
humanitarian concern can imprison human lives" (*Bury My Heart,* 67). Clearly,
the novel derives from Wells in its use of spatial enclosure to suggest social
restriction (Cf. Tom Henighan, *Natural Space in Literature* [Ottawa: Golden
Dog, 1982], 168–73). Although their backgrounds differed, neither Wells nor
Aldiss were members of the privileged British establishment.

6.   Henighan, *Natural Space in Literature,* 44–45.

7.   Cf. C. S. Lewis, *Out of the Silent Planet* (London: John Lane, 1938)
and its successors.

8.   This notion that the real cruelty might lie "out there" reverses the
trend inspired by the famous C. S. Lewis trilogy and referred to in Lewis's conversation with Aldiss and Amis (Cf. "Unreal Estates," 13).

9.   On the starship, as Collings notes, "immaturity is ritualized" (*Brian
W. Aldiss,* 11).

10.   Griffin, Collings, and Jameson, however, overlook the shallow character development and concentrate on elucidating the complex metaphors presented by the narrative.

11. As Griffin and Wingrove note in *Apertures* (42–43), Aldiss's World War II experience in the Far East had not been wasted. J. G. Ballard's experiences in Asia have also been related to his lush descriptive fiction. The landscapes of *Hothouse* are in fact much more cleanly rendered, less indulgent than most of Ballard's tropical scenes.

12. Aldiss, *Hothouse: A Science Fiction Novel* (London: Faber & Faber, 1962), 18. Hereafter cited in the text as *Hothouse*.

13. Griffin and Wingrove, *Apertures,* 51.

14. Mathews, *Aldiss Unbound,* 19.

15. *Hothouse* is close to alternate world science fiction, since Aldiss's future earth is so extreme as to cross the boundaries of reasonable extrapolation from present scientific knowledge. The premise of the sun entering a nova phase is not enough to account for the weirdnesses of the *Hothouse* world. And beyond question, the vertical dimension of story is of little importance here compared with the horizontal dimension of "world." In fact, the novel ends pretty much as it began, with the human bands going their separate ways, neither with much hope of experiencing anything other than what they have already experienced.

16. It is, however, also so extreme as to enable us to categorize *Hothouse*, in Malmgren's terms, as speculative rather than extrapolative. Cf. Malmgren, *Worlds Apart,* 12, 50.

17. Cf. John Wyndham's *The Day of the Triffids* (New York: Doubleday, 1951). Aldiss has generally condescended to Wyndham in print, but Wyndham's sense of the mood of the time and his ability to embody telling images in sharply focused and efficient narratives deserves more respect. His best books will certainly outlast Aldiss's worst.

18. Mathews, *Aldiss Unbound,* 44; *Bury My Heart,* 122.

19. Cf. also Crazy Jane's "For love has pitched his mansion in the place of excrement" ("Crazy Jane Talks to the Bishop," in *The Collected Poems of W. B. Yeats* (London: Macmillan, 1955), 294–95. As Mathews notes (*Aldiss Unbound,* 12), internal and external are here once again contrasted by Aldiss. But with what literalness! Wingrove and Griffin take this novel far too seriously (*Apertures,* 72–77). The best comments are by Collings (*Brian W. Aldiss,* 21–23).

20. Aldiss has some hilarious comments on this disparity in *Bury My Heart* (164–65).

21. This stagnation sets up a very difficult problem for the novelist, who—as E. M. Forster and others have reminded us—must deal with time. In fact, the clash between Aldiss's desire to portray a changeless society and the natural and personal need to evolve a story ("Narrative is what chiefly interests me in writing. I am a cause-and-effect addict," *Bury My Heart,* 204) is one of the things that sinks *The Malacia Tapestry.* Patrick Parrinder (*Science Fiction: Its Criticism and Teaching* [London, Methuen, 1980], 24–27) questions whether *The Malacia Tapestry* is science fiction at all.

22. The novelist Nina Bawden wrote; "I tried to enjoy *The Malacia Tapestry*. Brian Aldiss writes with such zest and gaiety that it seemed ungracious if not downright priggish, to be bored by his energetic tale, 'People appreciate merit only on a pretentious scale,' could be the author's clever way of thumbing his nose at the public. Or an unintentional criticism of his prancing, rich, but oddly tiring book" (quoted in Margaret Aldiss, *The Work of Brian W. Aldiss,* 304). What she is experiencing, quite probably, is the effect of the unresolved problem described previously (see n. 21).

23. A well-known and popular English translation of Dimitri Merejkowsky's *The Romance of Leonardo da Vinci* was published by Random House, New York, in 1931.

24. Collings, *Brian W. Aldiss,* 56.

25. Aldiss, *Enemies of the System: A Tale of Homo Uniformis* (London: Jonathan Cape, 1978), 102. Hereafter cited in the text as *Enemies*.

26. *Apertures,* 216. David Wingrove's discussion of this novel is one of the best; he shrewdly points out that the novel is about the pros and cons of controlling the human "id" (*Science Fiction Source Book,* 218). And although one might question Wingrove's notion that *Enemies* is a "direct homage" to Milton's *Paradise Lost* (219), the novel is certainly an attempt to "define in what manner Homo Uniformis has maimed itself in its attempt to make itself a wholly rational, controlled being" (217).

27. Aldiss, *Detached Retina,* 201–2.

Chapter Three

1. The *Helliconia* books, although lauded by reviewers, are still far from popular with science fiction fans. My own private survey indicates that many readers have simply not attempted to get through the series. If the World Wide Web (1998) may be taken as an indicator of current taste, we find few comments there about *Helliconia,* and the ones that exist are of an extremely derogatory nature. At this writing, however, an elaborate Web site created by Harper Collins Publishers to promote the *Helliconia* books is still in existence.

2. Aldiss, *Helliconia Spring* (London: Triad/Grafton, 1983), 5. Other references to *Helliconia* are from the separate volumes: *Helliconia Summer* (London: Triad/Grafton, 1985) and *Helliconia Winter* (London: Triad/Grafton, 1986). Hereafter cited in the text as *Spring, Summer, Winter,* respectively.

3. This is not to argue that this theme is the only one in the *Helliconia* books. Aldiss himself emphasizes the ecological side and writes that "of course, *Helliconia* is also a story of light, the glorious light without which we are nothing" (*Bury My Heart,* 176). One might legitimately connect the Aldiss novel with an important tradition by analyzing the imagery that recalls Percy Shelley's "Hymn of Apollo," contrasting it with the "Darkness" evoked by Lord Byron in his proto-science fiction poem of that name. The archetypal opposites

of darkness and light permeate Aldiss's *Helliconia* novels. See also Collings, *Brian W. Aldiss,* 70–76, for a brief but telling treatment of the linguistic and mythological aspects of the series.

4.   James E. Lovelock, *Gaia: A New Look at Life on Earth* (New York: Oxford University Press, 1979).

5.   See Richard D. Mullen, "The Earthmanist Culture: Cities in Flight as a Spenglerian History," in James Blish, *Cities in Flight* (New York: Avon, 1970), 597–607.

6.   As of 1998, Toynbee's influence is in recession, but at the time the *Helliconia* books were gestating in Aldiss's mind he was regarded as a major world thinker, and his *Study* became a touchstone of intellectual discussion about civilization during the period from about 1950–1970. In *Trillion Year Spree,* Aldiss mentions the Toynbean influence on the last volumes of Isaac Asimov's *Foundation,* but in his literary autobiography he mentions as an influence on *Helliconia* not Toynbee but another British historian, J. M. Roberts, whose book, *The Hutchinson History of the World,* and whose television series, "The Triumph of the West," Aldiss specifically credits with providing "a good idea of how civilization would continue" (*Bury My Heart,* 174–75).

7.   Arnold Toynbee, *A Study of History* (London: Oxford University Press, 1934–1961), vol. 1. Subsequent references are cited in the text by volume number.

8.   Both of which Toynbee considers under the notion of an Hellenic civilization. On the breakdown of classical civilization, see especially the chapters on "Schism in the Soul" in Toynbee, 5.

9.   Toynbee, 7. These higher religions he calls "Universal Churches."

10.   See "The Immanent Will Returns—2" in Aldiss, *Detached Retina,* 37–43 and also *Bury My Heart,* 176 and 189.

11.   Marvin Perry, *Arnold Toynbee and the Crisis of the West* (Washington, D.C.: Washington University Press, 1981), 123.

12.   Quoted in Jack G. Voller, "Universal Mindscape: The Gaia Hypothesis in Science Fiction," in George E. Slusser and Eric Rabkin, *Mindscapes: The Geographies of Imagined Worlds* (Carbondale: Southern Illinois University Press, 1989), 144.

13.   Popular histories that might have influenced him include: Gordon Childe, *What Happened in History* (Harmondsworth: Penguin, 1942), and W. H. McNeil, *The Rise of the West: A History of the Human Community* (Chicago: University of Chicago Press, 1963).

14.   Perry, *Arnold Toynbee,* 22.

15.   Perry, *Arnold Toynbee,* 18.

16.   See the works of Carl Jung, especially *Civilization in Transition: Collected Works,* vol. 10 (London: Routledge & Kegan Paul, 1964), and Lewis Mumford, *The Transformations of Man* (New York: Harper, 1956), both of whom Aldiss credits as influences on his thinking.

17. See Aldiss's *The Eighty-Minute Hour,* which comically dramatizes the same predicament.

18. Perry, *Arnold Toynbee,* 17.

19. For apocalyptic thinking see Mircea Eliade, *Myth and Reality* (New York: Harper, 1963) and *Cosmos and History: The Myth of the Eternal Return* (New York: Harper, 1954).

20. Frederick A. Kreuzinger, *Apocalypse and Science Fiction: A Dialectic of Religious and Secular Soteriologies* (Chico, Calif.: Scholar's Press, 1982), 49. See also David Ketterer, *New Worlds for Old: The Apocalyptic Imagination, Science Fiction and American Literature* (New York: Anchor, 1974).

21. Denise Terrel, *"Au Coeur du Labyrinthe: Le Phagor dans la Trilogie de Helliconia de Brian Aldiss," Études Anglaises* 41 (1988): 307–17.

22. J. Adam Frisch and Joseph Martos, "Religious Imagination and Imagined Religion," in Robert Reilly, ed. *The Transcendent Adventure: Studies of Religion in Science Fiction/Fantasy* (Westport, Conn.: Greenwood Press,, 1985), 20.

23. James Hastings Nichols, "Jacob Burckhardt," an introduction to Jacob Burckhardt, *Force and Freedom: An Interpretation of History* (New York: Pantheon, 1955), 34–39.

24. Voller, "Universal Mindscape," 148.

25. Perry, *Arnold Toynbee,* 91.

26. Voller, "Universal Mindscape," 148.

27. Griffin and Wingrove, *Apertures,* 230.

28. Cf. the final paragraph of Stapledon's *Last and First Men* (New York: Dover, 1968). The same novel offers another form of the Stapledonian "resignation" that infuriated C. S. Lewis. Cf. "Preparing a New World" in chapter 12, in which humanity joyously celebrates its massacre of an intelligent species on Venus.

Chapter Four

1. In Hatherley, *A is For Brian,* 50.

2. Aldiss has collected this work with his short stories, but it is clearly a short novel and must be considered with the longer fiction.

3. Henighan, *Natural Space in Literature,* 162.

4. As Aldiss has explained, the title of the story and the odd image of the saliva tree itself have little or nothing to do with the novel (*Bury My Heart,* 124–25).

5. Peter Hutchinson, *Games Authors Play* (London: Methuen, 1983), 92–95.

6. Aldiss, *Bury My Heart,* 97.

7. Aldiss and Harrison, *Hell's Cartographers,* 198–99. See also *Bury My Heart* (96–98), where Aldiss explains that *Report* was influenced by Heisenberg's idea of the Uncertainty Principle and the notion of the influence of the

observer. "I sat down to construct a fiction in which everything was observation, and no ultimate reference point existed," he writes. Aldiss goes on to note that the Holman Hunt painting is in fact the only relatively stable reference point in the story, but that it is described differently each time and is therefore also ultimately unstable.

8. Merril, *England Swings SF,* 9.

9. Aldiss describes *Report* as one of "three books which earned me hatred from American readers." (The other two were *Barefoot in the Head* and *Billion Year Spree.) Bury My Heart,* 98.

10. *Bury My Heart,* 99.

11. Aldiss and Harrison, *Hell's Cartographers,* 199. In *Apertures,* Brian Griffin makes a valiant case for this novel, introducing—somewhat surprisingly—the work of C. S. Lewis and Ray Bradbury as literary analogues. "But for all the minor faults of *Probability A,* there is no central ineptness on Aldiss's part," Griffin writes (Griffin and Wingrove, *Apertures,* 145). It is not a question of ineptness, of course, but of interest. Why should the reader be interested in what Griffin calls the "extremely limited actions" of vague characters "described in characteristic detail"? "The cumulative effect on the reader," Griffin asserts, "can be described thus; gradual fascination, then deepening hypnotic attention, graduating in to boredom and grim determination" (*Apertures,* 137).

But why *graduating?* The boredom is real and sustained, and no amount of special pleading can rescue this inert novel from the limbo in which Aldiss grimly, and with huge intellectual miscalculation, lodged it. Nonetheless, Collings describes it as a "major achievement." suggesting that it is a "classic statement on objectivity and the difficulty of interpretation" (*Brian W. Aldiss,* 32–35). "With a little effort, the book's puzzling edges can be got round," writes Richard Mathews in *Aldiss Unbound* (40). Mathews's analysis is perhaps the most straightforward and undefensive of all; he emphasizes both that the novel is centered on multiple "interruptions" in the reader's perception and that it is circular in form. These analyses perhaps serve to remind us that the fact that an artwork can be intellectually justified does not guarantee that the work in question will communicate pleasure and insight, even to a receptive audience. And ultimately, the latter is the most important factor in the survival of any work. The best overall study of Aldiss's work of this period is Colin Greenland's in *The Entropy Exhibition* (69–91), in which he emphasizes the instability and the dissonant elements in Aldiss's fictional reality.

12. Mathews, *Aldiss Unbound,* 41.

13. Willis E. McNelly describes the painting in terms of a "freeze-frame," in which a single moment isolated in time represents all time. In *Report,* Aldiss is, McNelly asserts, "unrelentingly visual" ("Report of Probability A," in Frank N. Magill, *Survey of Science Fiction* [Englewood Cliffs, 1979], 1766).

14. Goethe's comment is clearly a part of the philosophical dialogue then being carried on in the wake of the ideas of the German idealist philoso-

phers—the riposte of an artist to the Kantian complexifying of the process of knowing and not—except in a very limited sense—a prescription for art.

15. Quoted in Margaret Aldiss, *Work of Brian W. Aldiss,* 299.

16. Quoted in Richard Taruskin, "Why Do They All Hate Horowitz?" *The New York Times,* Sunday, November 28, 1993, H31.

17. For the order of composition, see *Bury My Heart,* 97–100; Aldiss and Harrison, *Hell's Cartographers,* 198–200; and Mathews, *Aldiss Unbound,* 35.

18. Mathews, *Aldiss Unbound,* 35–36.

19. Mathews, *Aldiss Unbound,* 37.

20. One of the clearest expositions of Guardieff's thought is in P. D. Ouspensky, *The Fourth Way* (New York: Vintage, 1971).

21. Mathews, *Aldiss Unbound,* 44.

22. Mathews, *Aldiss Unbound,* 46.

23. Aldiss, *Barefoot in the Head: A European Fantasia* (London: Faber & Faber, 1969), 244.

24. John Briggs, *Fractals: The Pattern of Chaos* (New York: Simon & Schuster, 1992).

25. Briggs, *Fractals,* 22–41.

26. See James Gleick, *Chaos: Making a New Science* (New York: Viking, 1987).

27. Ihab Hassan, *The Postmodern Turn* (Columbus: Ohio State University Press, 1987), 167–87.

28. Aldiss and Harrison, *Hell's Cartographers,* 200.

29. Aldiss, *Frankenstein Unbound* (London: Jonathan Cape, 1973), 124. Hereafter cited in the text as *Unbound.*

30. In my view Brian Griffin and David Wingrove sin badly in this regard. See Wingrove in *Apertures* (162–69). Other astonishing over-valuations occur. Nicholas Ruddick ("The Brood of Mary: Brian Aldiss, Frankenstein and Science Fiction," reprinted in *Bury My Heart,* 209–20) writes, for example, that "In *Frankenstein Unbound* Aldiss has created an alternate world in which his time-torn surrogate, Bodenland, comes to discover the nature of his psychological and cultural predicament through knowledge, in both the epistemological and biblical senses of the word, of Mary Shelley, the woman who first warned the children of the Enlightenment that the monster had been unbound" (216). This is rather like saying that in the comic strip Superman comes to deep psychological knowledge of his Oedipal conflicts, or that Odysseus achieves in *The Odyssey* a Proustian awareness of the passage of time. Patrick G. McLeod ("Frankenstein: Unbound and Otherwise," *Extrapolation* 21, no. 2) interprets some of Bodenland's seemingly unmotivated actions in terms of his desire to prevent the future from taking place. But this interpretation is ironically framed, since Bodenland "becomes what he seeks to destroy, even as he tries to destroy what he has become." Yet, in purely novelistic terms, Aldiss completely fails to produce anything more than a sketch for the transformations with which Ruddick, McLeod, and other critics obligingly credit him.

31. Quoted in Margaret Aldiss, *Work of Brian W. Aldiss,* 303.

32. "When I placed my head upon the pillow," Mary writes, "I did not sleep, nor could I be said to think. My imagination, unbidden, possessed and guided me, gifting the successive images that arose in my mind with a vividness far beyond the usual bounds of reverie" (Shelley, *Frankenstein,* ed. Rieger, 227. This description of the hypnagogic state is exact and powerful.

33. Leonard Maltin describes the film as a "thoroughly expendable horror outing" and suggests that the "capable cast goes slumming in schlockmeister Corman's first directorial effort in nearly twenty years" (*Leonard Maltin's 1996 Movie and Video Guide* [New York: Penguin, 1995], 460). Other popular film guides rate *Frankenstein Unbound* no higher. See also *Bury My Heart* (197–98).

34. The influence of Philip K. Dick is paramount here, as noted in Griffin and Wingrove, *Apertures,* 173.

35. Aldiss, *The Eighty-Minute Hour: A Space Opera* (Garden City, N.Y.: Doubleday, 1974), 13. Hereafter cited in the text as *Hour.*

36. Griffin and Wingrove, *Apertures,* 175. Curiously enough, the authors dismiss *The Eighty-Minute Hour* as "a work of criticism and not a novel at all," perhaps understandably missing the postmodern aesthetic in their 1984 analysis. To this reader it seems odd to dismiss this delightful novel as mere criticism while rating the wooden and in-the-head text of *Frankenstein Unbound* as a literary success. Richard Mathews (*Aldiss Unbound,* 54–56) is much more positive about *The Eighty-Minute Hour.*

37. See Collings in *Brian W. Aldiss,* 54–56.

38. Mathews, *Aldiss Unbound,* 59–60.

39. Aldiss, *Moreau's Other Island: A Novel* (London: Jonathan Cape, 1980), 39. Hereafter cited in the text as *Island.*

40. *The Male Response* of 1961 and *Moreau's Other Island* (1980) make an interesting comparison; the distance between them suggests not only the maturation of Aldiss's art, but the radical change in literature from a colonial to a postcolonial perspective.

41. Alan Watts and the sixties movements had by this time infiltrated the general culture. Cf. the sexual program in Watts's *Nature, Man and Woman* (New York: Pantheon, 1958), which by the 1980s seemed mainstream rather than marginal. The relevant Lévi-Strauss work is *Tristes Tropiques* (London: Jonathan Cape, 1973).

Chapter Five

1. See "Well Water," in Randall Jarrell, *The Complete Poems* (New York: Farrar, Straus, Giroux, 1969), 300.

2. The novel is based on Aldiss's experience in the Sanders' and Parker's bookstores in Oxford (*Bury My Heart,* 11–40).

3. *Bury My Heart,* 41–42, 55–56.

4.   D. B. Wyndham Lewis, *Rotting Hill* (Santa Barbara: Black Sparrow, 1986), among other things, deals savagely with traditional British stereotypes.

5.   Griffin and Wingrove, *Apertures,* 63.

6.   Aldiss continues to value these novels very highly (See *Bury My Heart,* 155ff.). "The *Horatio Stubbs Saga* is about a young man redeemed by the love of a bad woman—well, several bad women, to be honest." It is difficult, however, to see any rendering of "love" in these novels. "Redemption" is also a term that does not seem appropriate for the Stubbs novels. It is interesting to note that Aldiss wrote the first of the Stubbs novels at the height of his most self-indulgent period, just when he was beginning *Barefoot in the Head* (*Bury My Heart,* 156). *The Hand-Reared-Boy* might be said to be self-indulgent to the point of artistic self-destructiveness. Incredibly, the editor who objected to Aldiss's unredeemed sexual descriptions was named Robert (later Sir Robert) Lusty! (*Bury My Heart,* 157).

7.   Aldiss complains in good-humored fashion about the fact that no film was made of the Stubbs novels, even though the first two of the series made the best-seller lists. In the case of *The Hand-Reared-Boy,* this oversight is blamed on the masturbation scenes (*Bury My Heart,* 158–59). The point Aldiss seems to miss—when noting that media puritanism avoids dealing with masturbation but accepts all kinds of lurid violence—is that there is almost nothing else to film *but masturbation* in the first Stubbs novel. If *The Hand-Reared-Boy* had any substantial texture or story, a film would not have been out of the question, but, in fact, with the masturbation scenes gone, almost nothing remains.

8.   See Fraser Harrison, *The Dark Angel: Aspects of Victorian Sexuality* (London: Sheldon, 1979) and Wayland Young, *Eros Denied* (London: Weidenfeld & Nicolson, 1964). Young argues for sexual liberation but presents a very different scenario for creative sexuality in art and life than is encompassed in the Aldiss Stubbs novels. Maureen Duffy in *The Erotic World of Fairy* ([London: Hodder & Stoughton, 1972], 352), suggests that "science fiction exploits the technological idiom to produce something which is basically anti-scientific for as soon as anything can be proved or done it ceases to be material for sci-fi. Brian Aldiss recognized this in turning from science fiction to masturbatory fantasy after the moon landing." While this statement needs strong qualification, it is interesting that Duffy perceives the first of the Stubbs novels as a vehicle of masturbatory fantasy rather than taking it seriously as fiction.

9.   Aldiss and Harrison, *Hell's Cartographers,* 200.

10.   Aldiss, *A Rude Awakening* (London: Weidenfeld & Nicolson, 1978), 18. Hereafter cited in the text as *Awakening.*

11.   In his summary in *Apertures* (159), David Wingrove seems apologetic (understandably so) for the Stubbs novels, while in the same book (223–28), he discusses *Life in the West* as one of Aldiss's major fictions. Wingrove sees the main theme of the latter as Tom Squire's coming to terms with the schizophrenia of modern personal and social life; to Wingrove the

novel plays artfully with the themes of language and silence, a very plausible approach.

12.   Like Aldiss's Squire books, Ford's Tietjens novels describe the social and intellectual transformations of a whole era; however, they have the advantage of a continuous focus on the main character. Cf. *Parade's End* (New York: Knopf, 1966), first published between 1924 and 1928.

13.   The childhood material, for example, shows up in the relationship between Joseph Winter and his mother (*Bury My Heart,* 201).

14.   Aldiss here gets a dig in at the burgeoning popularity of fantasy (and possibly at the growing cults surrounding hugely successful female fantasy writers, such as Katherine Kurtz, Anne McCaffrey, and others).

15.   *Forgotten Life* (London: Victor Gollancz, 1988), 146.

16.   *Bury My Heart,* 184–87.

17.   Aldiss, *Remembrance Day* (London: Harper Collins, 1993), 13.

18.   Richard Hughes, *A High Wind in Jamaica* (New York: Signet, 1961), 183.

19.   Aldiss, *Somewhere East of Life* (New York: Carol & Graf, 1994), 355.

Chapter Six

1.   Says David Wingrove,: "Science fiction is essentially a short story form." (*Science Fiction Source Book,* 274).

2.   Malmgren, *Worlds Apart,* 7–17. On science fiction as myth, see Ursula K. Le Guin, *The Language of the Night* (New York: Putnam's, 1979), 73–82; Alexei and Cory Panshin, "Science Fiction and the Dimension of Myth," *Extrapolation* 22, no. 2 (1981): 125–39.

3.   *Bury My Heart,* 63.

4.   On the first collection, see Griffin and Wingrove, *Apertures,* 20–34, and Collings, *Brian W. Aldiss,* 78–82.

5.   Aldiss, "Outside," in *Best Science Fiction Stories of Brian Aldiss* (London: Gollancz, 1988), 17.

6.   Griffin and Wingrove, *Apertures,* 27–28.

7.   Margaret Aldiss, *Work of Brian W. Aldiss,* 150–54.

8.   Aldiss, "Who Can Replace a Man?" in *The Canopy of Time* (London: Faber & Faber, 1959), 50.

9.   "Super Toys" was for a long time a Stanley Kubrick film project. After many years of futile effort, Aldiss claims (in *Bury My Heart,* 196–97) to have found a way of translating the story into film (an intractable proposition, given the effectiveness of the story as a lyric cry)—and perhaps inevitably, the film has not so far been made.

10.   Aldiss, "The Small Stones of Tu Fu," in *A Romance of the Equator: Best Fantasy Stories* (London: Gollancz, 1989), 159.

11.   Aldiss, "The Blue Background," in *Seasons in Flight* (London: Jonathan Cape, 1984), 59.

12.   Also known as "Vietnam Encore," this story was written in response to a request for a Vietnam story from Jeanne van Buren Dann and Jack Dann and was first published in 1986 (See *Bury My Heart,* 110).

13.   *Billion Year Spree,* 244–45.

14.   I have chosen these anthologies among many in my own collection. All the anthologies mentioned were published in New York.

15.   For publication data of the Aldiss anthologies, see the bibliography.

16.   Aldiss, *Billion Year Spree,* 1.

17.   Aldiss, *Penguin Science Fiction Omnibus,* 11.

18.   Harlan Ellison, *Dangerous Visions* (New York: Doubleday, 1967), is the first of the much-lauded Ellison anthologies.

19.   Aldiss, *Detached Retina,* 70–81.

20.   He elaborates on this choice and qualifies it slightly in *Detached Retina,* 81ff.

21.   Brian Aldiss and David Wingrove, *Trillion Year Spree: The History of Science Fiction,* (London: Victor Gollancz, 1986), 273–274.

22.   Bennett, *The Journals of Arnold Bennett,* 3 vols. (London: Cassell, 1932–33) Volume I, 22–23. West, quoted on jacket blurb of Knut Hamsun, *Pan* (New York: Noonday Press, 1956).

Selected Bibliography

Primary Works

Novels

The Brightfount Diaries. London: Faber & Faber, 1955.

Non-Stop. London: Faber & Faber, 1958. Published in the United States as *Starship.* New York: Criterion, 1959.

Vanguard from Alpha. New York: Ace Books, 1959. With "Segregation" added, revised and reprinted in *Equator: A Human Time Bomb from the Moon!* London: Brown, Watson, Digit Book, 1961.

Bow Down to Nul. New York: Ace Books, 1960. Published in Britain as *The Interpreter.* London: Brown, Watson, Digit Book, 1961.

The Male Response: A Timely Original Story. New York: Galaxy Publishing, Beacon Books, 1961.

The Primal Urge. New York: Ballantine Books, 1961. Reprinted as *Minor Operation* in *New Worlds Science Fiction* 40 (June 1962): 4–54; 40 (July 1962): 67–121; and 40 (August 1962): 73–127.

Hothouse: A Science Fiction Novel. London: Faber & Faber, 1962. Published in the United States as *The Long Afternoon of Earth.* New York: New American Library, Signet Book, 1962.

The Dark Light Years: A Science Fiction Novel. London: Faber & Faber, 1964.

Greybeard. New York: Harcourt, Brace & World, 1964.

Earthworks: A Science Fiction Novel. London: Faber & Faber, 1965.

An Age. London: Faber & Faber, 1967. Published in the United States as *Cryptozoic!* Garden City, N.Y.: Doubleday, 1968.

Report on Probability A. London: Faber & Faber, 1968.

Barefoot in the Head: A European Fantasia. London: Faber & Faber, 1969.

The Hand-Reared Boy. London: Weidenfeld & Nicolson, 1970.

A Soldier Erect; or, Further Adventures of the Hand-Reared Boy. London: Weidenfeld & Nicolson, 1971.

Frankenstein Unbound. London: Jonathan Cape, 1973.

The Eighty-Minute Hour: A Space Opera. Garden City, N.Y.: Doubleday, 1974.

The Malacia Tapestry. London: Jonathan Cape, 1976.

Brothers of the Head. London: Pierrot Publishing, 1977. Reprinted with an additional story as *Brothers of the Head; and, Where the Lines Converge.* London: Panther, 1979.

Enemies of the System: A Tale of Homo Uniformis. London: Jonathan Cape, 1978.

A Rude Awakening. London: Weidenfeld & Nicolson, 1978.

Life in the West. London: Weidenfeld & Nicolson, 1980.

Moreau's Other Island: A Novel. London: Jonathan Cape, 1980. Published in the United States as *An Island Called Moreau: A Novel*. New York: Simon & Schuster, 1981.

Helliconia Spring. London: Jonathan Cape, 1982. Reprint, London: Triad/ Grafton, 1983.

Helliconia Summer. London: Jonathan Cape, 1983. Reprint, London: Triad/ Grafton, 1985.

Helliconia Winter. London: Jonathan Cape, 1985. Reprint, London: Triad/ Grafton, 1986.

The Year Before Yesterday: A Novel in Three Acts. New York: Franklin Watts, 1987. Published in Britain as *Cracken at Critical: A Novel in Three Acts*. Worcester Park, England: Kerosina Press, 1987.

The Magic of the Past. Worcester Park, England: Kerosina Press, 1987.

Ruins. London: Century Hutchinson, 1987.

Forgotten Life. London: Victor Gollancz, 1988.

The Saliva Tree. New York: Tor SF, Tom Doherty Associates Book, 1988. First separate publication of the novella.

Dracula Unbound. New York: Harper Collins, 1991.

Remembrance Day. London: Harper Collins, 1993.

Somewhere East of Life. London: Flamingo, 1994.

Story Collections

Space, Time, and Nathaniel. London: Faber & Faber, 1957.

The Canopy of Time. London: Faber & Faber, 1959.

No Time Like Tomorrow. New York: New American Library, Signet Book, 1959.

Galaxies Like Grains of Sand. New York: New American Library, Signet Book, 1960.

Equator: A Human Time Bomb from the Moon! London: Brown, Watson, Digit Book, 1961.

The Airs of Earth: Science Fiction Stories. London: Faber & Faber, 1963.

Starswarm. New York: New American Library, Signet Book, 1964.

Best Science Fiction Stories of Brian W. Aldiss. London: Faber & Faber, 1965. Published in the United States as *Who Can Replace a Man? The Best Science Fiction Stories of Brian W. Aldiss* New York: Harcourt, Brace & World, 1966.

The Saliva Tree and Other Strange Growths. London: Faber & Faber, 1966.

Intangibles, Inc., and Other Stories: Five Novellas. London: Faber & Faber, 1969.

A Brian Aldiss Omnibus, Containing : The Interpreter, The Primal Urge, The Saliva Tree, The Impossible Star, Basis for Negotiation, Man in His Time. London: Sidgwick & Jackson, 1969.

Neanderthal Planet. New York: Avon, 1970.

The Moment of Eclipse. London: Faber & Faber, 1970.

A Brian Aldiss Omnibus. Vol. 2. London: Sidgwick & Jackson, 1971. Contains *Space, Time, and Nathaniel, Non-Stop,* and *The Male Response.*

Best Science Fiction Stories of Brian W. Aldiss. Rev. ed. London: Faber & Faber, 1971.

The Book of Brian Aldiss. New York: DAW Books, 1972. Published in Britain as *The Comic Inferno.* London: New English Library, 1973.

Last Orders and Other Stories. London: Jonathan Cape, 1977.

Brothers of the Head; and, Where the Lines Converge. London: Panther, 1979.

New Arrivals, Old Encounters: Twelve Stories. London: Jonathan Cape, 1979.

Science Fiction Verhalen: Brian Aldiss. Utrecht, Antwerp: Prisma/Het Spectrum, 1979. Trans. Pon Ruiter. Dutch language collection.

Foreign Bodies: Stories. Singapore: Chopmen, 1981.

Dunkler Bruder Zukunft: Der Brian W. Aldiss-Reader. Bergisch Gladbach: Bastei Lubbe, 1982. German language collection.

Brian W. Aldiss. Ed. Maxim Jakubowski. Paris: Presses Poclet, 1982. French language collection.

Best of Aldiss. Bestsellers, vol. 3, no. 9. London: Viaduct Publications, 1983.

Seasons in Flight. London: Jonathan Cape, 1984.

The Horatio Stubbs Saga. London: Granada, 1985. Includes *The Hand-Reared Boy, A Soldier Erect,* and *A Rude Awakening.*

Kto Zastapi Czlowieka Warsawa: Iskry, 1985. Polish language collection.

Best Science Fiction Stories of Brian W. Aldiss. rev. ed. London: Victor Gollancz, 1988. Reprinted as *Man in His Time: Best SF Stories.* London: Gollancz VGSF, 1989, and *Man in His Time: The Best Science Fiction Stories of Brian W. Aldiss.* New York: Atheneum, 1989.

Science Fiction Blues: The Show That Brian Aldiss Took on the Road: A Selection of His Very Best Stories, Poetry, and Speculations: An Evening of Wonder. Ed. by Frank Hatherley. London: Avernus, 1988.

A Romance of the Equator: Best Fantasy Stories. London: Victor Gollancz, 1989.

Krazenie Krwi. Warszawa: Iskry, 1989. Trans. Robert M. Sadowski.

Bodily Functions: Four Stories, and a Letter to Sam on the Subject of Bowel Movement. London: Avernus, 1991.

The Secret of This Book. London: Harper Collins, 1995. Published in the United States as *Twenty Odd Stories.* New York: Harper Collins, 1995.

Poems

Pile: Petals from St. Klaed's Computer. Illustrated by Mike Wilks. London: Jonathan Cape, 1979.

Farewell to a Child: 10 Poems. Berkhamstead: Priapus Poets, 1982.

Stories and Papers

A Romance of the Equator. Birmingham: Birmingham SF Group for Novacon 10 in 1980.

The Life of Samuel Johnson, LL.D.: A Series of his Epistolatory Correspondence and Conversations with Many Eminent Persons, Never Before Published. Ed. [i.e. written] by Aldiss. Oxford: Printed by Christopher Munday for Oxford Polytechnic Press at Headington, 1980.

My Country 'Tis Not Only of Thee. Oxford: Aldiss Appreciation Society, 1987.

Sex and the Black Machine. London: Avernus, 1988.

Nonfiction

Cities and Stones: A Traveller's Jugoslavia. London: Faber & Faber, 1966.

The Shape of Further Things: Speculations on Change. London: Faber & Faber, 1970.

Billion Year Spree: The History of Science Fiction. London: Weidenfeld & Nicolson, 1973. Published in the United States with the subtitle *The True History of Science Fiction.* Garden City, N.Y.: Doubleday, 1973.

Hell's Cartographers: Some Personal Histories of Science Fiction Writers. Ed. with Harry Harrison, with contributions from Alfred Bester, Damon Knight, Frederik Pohl, Robert Silverberg, Harry Harrison, and Aldiss. London: Weidenfeld & Nicolson, SF Horizons, 1975.

Science Fiction Art: The Fantasies of SF. London: New English Library, 1975. Anthology.

Science Fiction Horizons. Vols. 1 and 2. Ed. and written with Harry Harrison and Tom Boardman. New York: Arno Press, 1975.

Science Fiction as Science Fiction. Frome, Somerset: Bran's Head Books, 1978. Collected essays.

This World and Nearer Ones: Essays Exploring the Familiar. London: Weidenfeld & Nicolson, 1979. Collected essays.

Science Fiction Quiz. London: Weidenfeld & Nicolson, 1983. Included in *The Penguin Master Quiz.* Harmondsworth, Middlesex: Penguin Books, 1985.

The Pale Shadow of Science. Seattle: Serconia Press, 1985. Collected essays.

. . . And the Lurid Glare of the Comet. Seattle: Serconia Press, 1986. Collected essays.

Trillion Year Spree: The History of Science Fiction. With David Wingrove. London: Victor Gollancz, 1986.

Bury My Heart at W. H. Smith's: A Writing Life. London: Hodder & Stoughton, 1990.

The Detached Retina: Aspects of Science Fiction and Fantasy. Syracuse, N.Y.: Syracuse University Press, 1995.

The Twinkling of an Eye: My Life as an Englishman. London: Little, Brown, 1998.

When the Feast is Finished. London: Little Brown, 1999.

Edited Anthologies

Penguin Science Fiction: An Anthology. Harmondsworth: Penguin Books, 1961.

Best Fantasy Stories. London: Faber & Faber, 1962.

More Penguin Science Fiction: An Anthology. Harmondsworth: Penguin Books, 1963.

Introducing SF: A Science Fiction Anthology. London: Faber & Faber, 1964.

Yet More Penguin Science Fiction: An Anthology. Harmondsworth: Penguin Books, 1964.

Science Fiction Horizons, ed. with Harry Harrison. New York: Arno Press, 1975. Facsimile edition in one volume of the only two issues of *SF Horizons* Magazine, 1964–1965.

Nebula Award Stories Two. Ed. with Harry Harrison. Garden City, N.Y.: Doubleday, 1967.

Best SF: 1967. Ed. with Harry Harrison. New York: Berkley Medallion Books, 1968. Published in Britain as *The Year's Best Science Fiction.* No. 1. London: Sphere Books, 1968.

Farewell, Fantastic Venus! A History of the Planet Venus in Fact and Fiction. Assisted by Harry Harrison. London: Macdonald, 1968. Published in the United States as *All About Venus: A Revelation of the Planet Venus in Fact and Fiction.* New York: Dell, 1968.

Best SF: 1968. Ed. with Harry Harrison. New York: G. P. Putnam's Sons, 1969. Published in Britain as *The Year's Best Science Fiction.* No. 2. London: Sphere Books, 1969.

Best SF: 1969. Ed. with Harry Harrison. New York: G. P. Putnam's Sons, 1970. Published in Britain as *The Year's Best Science Fiction.* No. 3. London: Sphere Books, 1970.

Best SF: 1970. Ed. with Harry Harrison. New York: G. P. Putnam's Sons, 1971. Published in Britain as *The Year's Best Science Fiction.* No. 4. London: Sphere Books, 1971.

Best SF: 1971. Ed. with Harry Harrison. New York: G. P. Putnam's Sons, 1972. Published in Britain as *The Year's Best Science Fiction.* No. 5. London: Sphere Books, 1972.

The Astounding-Analog Reader. Vol. 1. Ed. with Harry Harrison. Garden City, N.Y.: Doubleday, 1972.

The Astounding-Analog Reader. Vol. 2. Ed. with Harry Harrison, Garden City, N.Y.: Doubleday, 1973.

Best SF: 1972. Ed. with Harry Harrison. New York: G. P. Putnam's Sons, 1973. Published in Britain as *The Year's Best Science Fiction.* No. 6. London: Sphere Books, 1973.

The Penguin Science Fiction Omnibus: An Anthology. Harmondsworth: Penguin Books, 1973. Contains *Penguin Science Fiction, More Penguin Science Fiction, Yet More Penguin Science Fiction.*

Best SF: 1973. Ed. with Harry Harrison. New York: G. P. Putnam's Sons, 1974. Published in Britain as *The Year's Best Science Fiction.* No. 7. London: Sphere Books, 1975.

Space Opera: An Anthology of Way-Back-When Futures. London: Weidenfeld & Nicolson, 1974.

Best SF: 1974. Ed. with Harry Harrison. Indianapolis: Bobbs-Merril, 1975.
Published in Britain as *The Year's Best Science Fiction.* No. 8. London:
Sphere Books, 1975.
Space Odysseys: An Anthology of Way-Back-When Futures. London: Weidenfeld &
Nicolson, 1975. Published in the United States with the subtitle *A New
Look at Yesterday's Futures.* Garden City, N.Y.: Doubleday, 1976.
Decade: The 1940s. Ed. with Harry Harrison. London: Macmillan, 1975.
Evil Earths: An Anthology of Way-Back-When Futures. London: Weidenfeld &
Nicolson, 1975.
Best SF: 75, the Ninth Annual. Ed. with Harry Harrison. Indianapolis: Bobbs-
Merril, 1976. Published in Britain as *The Year's Best Science Fiction.* No. 9.
London: Futura Publications, Orbit Book, 1976.
Decade: The 1950s. Ed. with Harry Harrison. London: Macmillan, 1976.
Galactic Empires: An Anthology of Way-Back-When Futures. London: Futura Publi-
cations, Orbit Book, 1976.
Decade: The 1960s. Ed. with Harry Harrison. London: Macmillan, 1977.
Perilous Planets: An Anthology of Way-Back-When Futures. London: Weidenfeld &
Nicolson, 1978.
The Penguin Science Fiction Omnibus. London: Penguin, 1974.
The Penguin World Omnibus of Science Fiction. Ed, with Sam J. Lundwall. Har-
mondsworth, Middlesex: Penguin Books, 1986.
My Madness: The Selected Writings of Anna Kavan. London: Picador Classics, 1990.

Secondary Works

Books

Aldiss, Margaret. *The Work of Brian W. Aldiss: An Annotated Bibliography and
Guide.* Edited by Boden Clarke. San Bernardino, Calif.: R. Reginald,
Borgo Press, 1992. An indispensable tool for the study of Aldiss's work.
Includes a brief autobiographical afterward and copious annotations by
Aldiss himself.
Collings, Michael R. *Brian W. Aldiss.* Starmont Reader's Guide 28. Mercer
Island, Wash.: Starmont House, 1986. A decade-by-decade survey of
Aldiss's fiction through the 1980s, uniformly sensitive and intelligent.
Greenland, Colin. *The Entropy Exhibition: Michael Moorcock and the British "New
Wave" in Science Fiction,* 69–92. London: Routledge & Kegan Paul, 1983.
The indispensable book on the subject, with a good chapter on Aldiss,
emphasizing the unresolved tensions in his fiction.
Griffin, Brian, and David Wingrove. *Apertures: A Study of the Writings of Brian
Aldiss.* Contributions to the Study of Science Fiction & Fantasy, no. 8.

Westport, Conn.: Greenwood Press, 1984. The most comprehensive critical work on Aldiss so far. The two writers, one a collaborator with Aldiss
in *Trillion Year Spree,* in alternative chapters explore the Aldiss oeuvre up
to the early 1980s. The book is vastly informed but overzealous in relating Aldiss's work to the intellectual currents of the time, a practice that
often results in overevaluations of the fiction.

Hatherley, Frank. *A is for Brian: A 65th Birthday Present for Brian W. Aldiss from
His Family, Friends, Colleagues, and Admirers.* London: Avernus, 1990. This
tribute contains some valuable biographical material and a very interesting essay on Aldiss and his work by Christopher Priest.

Mathews, Richard. *Aldiss Unbound: The Science Fiction of Brian W. Aldiss.* The
Milford Series: Popular Writers of Today, vol. 9. San Bernardino, Calif.:
Borgo Press, 1977. A long monograph covering Aldiss's fiction up to end
of the 1970s. Helpful on Aldiss's new wave novels.

Articles and Parts of Books

Bakes, Roger Francis. "Brian Aldiss and His Approaches to the Science-Fiction
Tradition." Master's thesis, Department of English, University of Cal-
gary, Alberta, Canada, 1987.

Barbour, Douglas. "Aldiss, Brian (Wilson)." In *Twentieth-Century Science-Fiction
Writers,* ed. Curtis C. Smith. New York: St. Martin's Press; London:
Macmillan, 1981. A brief but useful note on Aldiss's work.

Blish, James and Brian W. Aldiss. "In Conversation: James Blish Talks to Brian
Aldiss." *Vector* 63 (January–February 1973): 6–17. Interview.

Colbert, Robert E. "Unbinding Frankenstein: The Science Fiction Criticism of
Brian Aldiss." *Extrapolation* 23 (Winter 1982): 333–44.

Collings, Michael R. "Brian W. Aldiss—Cartographer." Paper submitted to the
Fifth International Conference on the Fantastic in the Arts, Florida
Atlantic University, Boca Raton, March 1984.

Crispin, Edmund. "Brian Aldiss: The Image Maker." *New Worlds Science Fiction*
154 (September 1965): 3–11. Critique.

Eckley, Grace. "Barefoot in the Head." In *Survey of Science Fiction Literature,* ed.
Frank N. Magill, 125–29. Englewood Cliffs, N.J.: Salem Press, 1979. A
brief summary and positive evaluation of the novel.

Elliot, Jeffrey M. "An Interview with Brian Aldiss." *Future Life* 21 (September
1980): 44–46, 67.

Fleming, Linda. "The American SF Sub-Culture." *Science Fiction Studies* 4, pt. 3
(November 1977): 263–71.

Gillespie, Bruce. "Cryptozoic." In *Survey of Science Fiction Literature,* ed. Frank N.
Magill, 443–47. Englewood Cliffs, N.J.: Salem Press, 1979. A brief
summary and evaluation.

————. "Greybeard." In *Survey of Science Fiction Literature*, ed. Frank N. Magill, 926–31. Englewood Cliffs, N.J.: Salem Press, 1979. A brief summary and evaluation of the novel.

————. "Literature Which Awakens Us: The Science Fiction of Brian W. Aldiss." In *The Stellar Gauge: Essays on Modern Science Fiction Writers,* ed. Michael J. Tolley and Kirpal Singh. Carlton, Victoria: Nostrilia Press, 1980.

Goddard, James. "Interrogation: Brian Aldiss Answers Questions." *Cypher* 6 (January 1972): 6–21. Interview.

Gordon, Richard. "Brian W. Aldiss: A Man in His Time." *Speculation* 2 (September 1968): 15–23. Critique. Greenland, Colin. "Aldiss, Brian W." In *Dictionary of Literary Biography: British Novelists Since 1960*, 2 vols. (Detroit: Gale, 1983): 3–18.

————. "The Times Themselves Talk Nonsense: Language in *Barefoot in the Head*." *Foundation* 17 (1979): 32–41. Critique.

Griffin, Brian. "Inside/Outside." *Kipple* 2 (October 1978).

————. "Moving Towards Chaos: Aldiss's Hothouse." *Foundation* 20 (October 1980): 15–27.

Harrison, Harry. "The Long Afternoon of Earth." In *Survey of Science Fiction Literature,* ed. Frank N. Magill, 1235–37. Englewood Cliffs, N.J.: Salem Press, 1979.

I Romanzi Fantascientifici di Brian W. Aldiss. Master's thesis, Universita degli studi di Milano, 1981.

Jameson, Frederic. "Generic Discontinuities in SF: Brian Aldiss's *Starship*." *Science-Fiction Studies* 1, no. 2 (Fall 1973): 57–68. Critique. An important essay.

Lawson, Nicholas. "Talking to the Aliens: Language in the Stories of Brian Aldiss." *The Incorporated Linguist* 2, 3, 4 (1984): 236–37.

McLeod, Patrick G. "Frankenstein: Unbound and Otherwise." *Extrapolation* 21 (1980): 158–66.

McNelly, William E. "Brian W. Aldiss, 1925—." In *Science Fiction Writers: Critical Studies of the Major Authors from the Early Nineteenth Century to the Present Day,* ed. E. F. Bleiler. New York: Charles Scribner's Sons, 1982.

————. "Frankenstein Unbound." In *Survey of Science Fiction Literature,* ed. Frank N. Magill, 840–44. Englewood Cliffs, N.J.: 1979. A brief analysis.

————. "Report on Probability A." In *Survey of Science Fiction Literature,* ed. Frank N. Magill, 1764–67. Englewood Cliffs, N.J.: 1979. A brief and positive evaluation of the novel.

McPharlin, John. "Aldiss Unzipped." *Australian Science Fiction Review* (1978): 117–26. Critique.

Ozolims, Aija. "Recent Work on Mary Shelley and *Frankenstein*." *Science-Fiction Studies* 3 (1976): 187–202. Critique.

Pringle, David. "Brian Aldiss: *The Malacia Tapestry.*" In *Modern Fantasy: The Hundred Best Novels: An English-Language Selection, 1946–1987.* London: Grafton Books, 1988.

————. "Brian W. Aldiss: *Greybeard.*" In *Science Fiction: The 100 Best Novels: An English-Language Selection, 1949–1984.* London: Xanadu, 1985.

————. "Brian W. Aldiss: *Hothouse.*" In *Science Fiction: The 100 Best Novels: An English-Language Selection, 1949–1984.* London: Xanadu, 1985.

————. "Brian W. Aldiss: *Non-Stop.*" In *Science Fiction: The 100 Best Novels: An English-Language Selection, 1949–1984.* London: Xanadu, 1985.

Sadler, Frank. "Report on Probability A." *The Unified Ring: Narrative Art and the Science-Fiction Novel.* Ann Arbor, Mich.: UMI Research Press, 1984. A detailed study of the novel, part of which is quoted by Aldiss in *Bury My Heart at W. H. Smith's.*

Tweng, Low Hwee. *The Science Fiction of Brian W. Aldiss: A Consideration of Three Novels.* Master's thesis, National University of Singapore, 1980.

Other Titles Consulted

Amis, Kingsley. *New Maps of Hell: A Survey of Science Fiction.* New York: Harcourt Brace, 1960.

————, ed. *The Golden Age of Science Fiction.* London: Hutchinson, 1981.

Bailey, J. O. *Pilgrims Through Space and Time.* 1947. Reprint, Westport, Conn.: Greenwood Press, 1972.

Borges, Jorge Luis. *Other Inquisitions.* Austin: University of Texas Press, 1964.

Briggs, John. *Fractals: The Patterns of Chaos.* New York: Simon and Schuster, 1992.

Childe, Gordon. *What Happened in History.* Harmondsworth: Penguin, 1942.

Clareson, Thomas D. *SF: The Other Side of Realism.* Bowling Green: Bowling Green University Press, 1971.

Conklin, Groff. *Possible Worlds of Science Fiction.* New York: Vanguard, 1951.

Derleth, August. *Beyond Time and Space: A Compendium of Science-Fiction Through the Ages.* New York: Pellegrini & Cudahy, 1950.

Ellison, Harlan. *Dangerous Visions.* New York: Doubleday, 1967.

Franklin, H. Bruce. *Future Perfect: American Science Fiction of the Nineteenth Century.* New York: Oxford University Press, 1978.

Gerber, Richard. *Utopian Fantasy.* New York: McGraw-Hill, 1973.

Goulart, Ron. *An Informal History of the Pulp Magazines.* New York: Ace, 1972.

Hassan, Ihab. *The Postmodern Turn: Essays in Postmodern Theory and Culture.* Columbus: Ohio State University Press, 1987.

Healey, Raymond J., and J. Francis McComas. *Adventures in Time and Space.* New York: Random House, 1946.

Hutchinson, Peter. *Games Authors Play.* London: Metheun, 1983.

Lawler, Donald. *Approaches to Science Fiction.* Boston: Houghton Mifflin, 1978.

Lewis, C. S. *Of Other Worlds: Essays and Stories.* London: Geoffrey Bes, 1966.

Lovelock, James E. *Gaia: A New Look at Life on Earth.* New York: Oxford University Press, 1979.

Lundwall, Sam J. *Science Fiction: What It's All About.* New York: Ace, 1971.

Malmgren, Carl D. *Worlds Apart.* Indianapolis: Indiana University Press, 1991.

McNeil, W. H. *The Rise of the West: A History of the Human Community.* Chicago: University of Chicago Press, 1963.

Merril, Judith. *England Swings SF.* New York: Ace, 1968.

Nicholls, Peter, ed. *The Encyclopedia of Science Fiction.* London: Granada, 1979.

Parrinder, Patrick: *Science Fiction: Its Criticism and Teaching.* London: Metheun, 1980.

Pratt, Fletcher. *World of Wonder.* New York: Twayne, 1951.

Rabkin, Eric S. *Fantastic Worlds: Myths, Tales and Stories.* New York: Oxford University Press, 1979.

Rose, Mark. *Alien Encounters: Anatomy of Science Fiction.* Cambridge, Mass.: Harvard University Press, 1981.

————, ed. *Science Fiction: A Collection of Critical Essays.* Englewood Cliffs, N.J.: Prentice Hall, 1976.

Rottensteiner, Franz. *The Science Fiction Book: An Illustrated History.* New York: Seabury Press, 1975.

Scholes, Robert, and Eric S. Rabkin. *Science Fiction: History, Science, Vision.* New York: Oxford University Press, 1977.

Shelley, Mary. *Frankenstein, or The Modern Prometheus*, ed. James Rieger. Indianapolis: Bobbs-Merril, 1974.

Slusser, George E., and Eric S. Rabkin., ed. *Mindscapes: The Geographies of Imagined Worlds.* Carbondale: Southern Illinois University Press, 1989.

Toynbee, Arnold. *Christianity Among the Religions of the World.* New York: Scribner's, 1957.

————. *A Study of History.* London: Oxford University Press, 1934–1961.

————. *The World and the West.* New York: Oxford University Press, 1953

Wingrove, David. *The Science Fiction Source Book.* New York: Van Nostrand-Reinhold, 1984.

Web Site

"The Official Brian W. Aldiss Web Site." Maintained by James Goddard. http://freespace.virgin.net/jim.g/BWA.

Index

Age, An (published in the United States as *Cryptozoic*), 68–70; comparison to *The Persistence of Memory:* Salvador Dali painting, 68–69; critical response to, 68; Jurassic Age in, 69; plot of, 69; publication of, 68; setting, 69; validation of science fiction writer's perspective 69–70

Airs of Earth, The, 112

Aldiss, Brian Wilson: American market for work of, 16; autobiography of, 110 *(see also Bury My Heart at W.H. Smith's);* career of, 2–10; 123–26; children of, 2; committees participated in, 2–3; as a critic, 63; critical response to work of *(see individual works);* early life of, 1–2; as an editor and reviewer, 2, 116–18; education of, 1; family background, 1–2; influence of Aldiss on world science fiction 3–4, 126; mainstream fiction, 90–108 *(see individual titles);* marriages of, 2; military service of, 1–2; as a performer, 3, 63; personality of, 63; physical appearance of, 2; postmodernism and, 63–89; 109. *(See also individual works);* as a prolific writer, 2–3, 8–9, 33–34, 109; science fiction of *(see individual works);* science fiction tradition and, 7–10; 109; short fiction of: 110–16; works as basis for films, 89

AWARDS RECEIVED

Hugo, with David Wingrove, for *Trillion Year Spree,* 3, 118

Hugo-winning stories, 19

Most Promising New Author (1958), 3

Nebula, 3, 64 *(see also The Saliva Tree and Other Strange Growths)*

Pilgrim Award, 3

Aldiss, Harry Hilyard, 1

Aldiss, Margaret Manson, 2

Aldiss, Stanley, 1

"All the World's Tears", 111 *(see also Canopy of Time, The)*

Amis, Kingsley, 19, 92

Anderson, Poul, 6

"Appearance of Life, An." See *Last Orders and Other Stories*

Asimov, Isaac, 6, 10, comparison of works to *Helliconia,* 61, popularity, 123

Astounding Science Fiction Magazine. See Campbell, John W.

Austen, Jane, 90

Bailey, J.O., *Pilgrims Through Space and Time,* 118

Ballard, J.G., 7, 8–9, 68

Barefoot in the Head, 64, 68–73; Aldiss's attitude to and writing time, 72; anti-psychiatry of R.D. Laing, 71; chaos theory, 72; communication, degeneration of, 71; compared to Samuel Beckett, 70; compared to Joyce's *Finnegan's Wake,* 71; connections of character Charteris to Leslie Charteris, Timothy Leary, and Charles Manson, 70; genre, 72; George Ivanovitch Guardieff's idea of awakening in, 70; language of, 71–72; mental degeneration, 70–71; postmodernism in, 72; science and art, new perspectives, 72; sixties drug culture, 70; social chaos, 70; surrealism, connection with, 71; violence, 70

Battlestar Galactica, 120

Beckett, Samuel, 70, 72

Bennett, Arnold, 92, 121

Bergson, Henri, 33

Best SF Stories:1965. See "Poor Little Warrior"

Best SF Stories:1988 , 110 *(see also Space, Time and Nathaniel)*

Best Science Fiction: The Decade: 1940s, 117; *The Decade: 1950s,* 117; *The Decade: 1960s,* 117

Billion Year Spree, 25, 26, 117–21, 120, 126; balance and range of, 118; compared to G.K. Chesterton's *The Victorian Age in Literature,* E. M. Forster's *Aspects of the Novel,* and Gilbert, Highet's *Poets in a Landscape,* 126

Blish, James: *Cities in Flight* compared to *Helliconia Series,* 61; as critic, 4; 8; inspired, like Aldiss, by historical structures, 39

Booker Prize Committee, 2

"Blue Background, The." See *Seasons in Flight*

Borges, Jorge Luis, 7, 8, 63

Bow Down to Nul (published in Britain as *The Interpreter),* 16

Boyer, Harold, 1

Bradbury, Ray, 110–11, 116

The Brightfount Diaries: 2, 90–92, 110, 126; compared to Kingsley Amis and Angry Young Men, 92; compared to Arnold Bennett, *Riceyman Steps,* 92; compared to George Grossmith, *Diary of A Nobody,* 92; compared to James Herriot, *All Things Great and Small,* 92; humor in, 91–92; narrative style, 91–92; setting, 90–91; postwar British fiction, relationship to, 92; compared to H.G. Wells, *Kipps,* 92

The Author

Tom Henighan, M. Litt. (Durham), Ph.D., Newcastle, is associate professor of English at Carleton University, Ottawa, Canada. He has published a novel, *The Well of Time* (shortlisted for the Bantam-Seal first novel award in 1986), two collections of stories, and a book of poetry. He was guest of honor at the Maplecon science fiction convention in Ottawa in 1982 and 1983. His 1976 television network lectures on science fiction were the first in Canada. In 1979, he produced the first Canadian performance of Karel Čapek's play, *RUR,* for which he was honored with a reception by the Czech embassy. Other publications include: *Brave New Universe: Testing the Values of Science in Society* (1980), *Natural Space in Literature* (1982), *The Presumption of Culture* (1996), and *Ideas of North: A Guide to Canadian Arts and Culture* (1997).

The Editor

Kinley E. Roby is professor emeritus of English at Northeastern University. He is the twentieth-century field editor of Twayne's English Authors Series, series editor of Twayne's Critical History of British Drama, and general editor of Twayne's Women and Literature Series. He has written books on Arnold Bennett, Edward VII, and Joyce Cary and has edited a collection of essays on T. S. Eliot. He makes his home in Naples, Florida.